MEN
OF THE
STARS

MEN
OF THE
STARS

PATRICK MOORE

B. Mitchell

Executive Manager	Kelly Flynn
Editorial Manager	Susan Egerton-Jones
Art Editor	Hans Verkroost
Editorial Assistant	Fiona Thomas
Production	Peter Phillips

Edited and designed by the Artists House
Division of Mitchell Beazley International Ltd.
Artists House
14–15 Manette Street
London W1V 5LB

"An Artists House Book"
© Mitchell Beazley Publishers 1986
© Text: Hester Myfanwy Woodward 1986

ISBN 0999922173

Typeset by Hourds Typographica Limited, Stafford.
Reproduction by La Cromolito s.n.c., Milan.
Printed in Italy by Poligrafici Calderara. s.p.a., Bologna.

CONTENTS

FOREWORD

How does one tell the story of a science? By discoveries, certainly; in astronomy nothing is easier. We can look back to Galileo's first views through a telescope, Isaac Newton watching the apple plummet from the tree, or Lord Rosse having his first sight of a spiral star-system; we can picture the bewilderment felt by the radio engineer Karl Jansky when he found that his makeshift aerial was picking up signals from the Milky Way; we can share in the triumph of the Russian space-planners when their football-sized Sputnik soared into the sky. But what about the men and women themselves? How did they go about their work, and what kinds of people were they?

What I hope to do, in this book, is to tell the story of astronomy not so much by hard fact as by personality. There is plenty to say, but the very early part of the story is not so easy to deal with, because the records are hopelessly incomplete, and what information we have is scientific rather than personal. Obviously the cave-men of the Ice Age looked up at the sky and marvelled at it, presumably regarding the Earth as the most important of all bodies and being served by the Sun and Moon, which were either gods or else places where the gods lived. There was, in fact, no reason for the mammoth-hunters to think otherwise. And when we come to consider the first "astronomers", we are little better off. Undoubtedly the Egyptians, the Chaldæans and the Chinese paved the way, and we do have a few names to help us, though whether any of them are authentic is quite another matter. It is really with the Greeks that we begin to have some positive information, so let us begin with the first of the great Greek philosophers, Thales of Miletus.

THALES
THE FIRST GREAT ASTRONOMER

An excellent additional reason for beginning with Thales is that we have at least a vague idea of his personality. Apparently he was a keen observer of the sky, and he was also a good businessman. From his scientific knowledge he guessed that in one particular year the olive crop would be poor—so he prudently bought up all the available groves, and when olives proved to be in short supply he "cashed in" handsomely. He was also associated with an eclipse, and it is for this that he is probably best remembered today.

An eclipse of the Sun is caused when the Moon passes in front of the brilliant solar disk, and blots it out for a short while. No total eclipse can last for as long as eight minutes, but the effect is spectacular; as soon as the last segment of the Sun is covered by the advancing Moon, the solar "atmosphere" flashes into view, and we see the red prominences and the glorious pearly "corona" which stretches out in all directions. Of course everything depends upon the lining-up being exact, and from any one position on Earth total eclipses are rare (the last to be seen over anywhere in England was in 1927; the next will not be until 1999). But there is a certain periodicity about them. After 18 years 11.3 days the Sun, Earth and Moon return to approximately the same relative positions, so that any one eclipse is apt to be followed by another one 18 years 11.3 days later—a cycle which is now known as the Saros. It is by no means perfect, but it is much better than nothing at all.

Thales knew about the Saros, and found that an eclipse was due on a definite date in 585 BC. At that time a war was in progress between the Lydians and the Medes, and from all

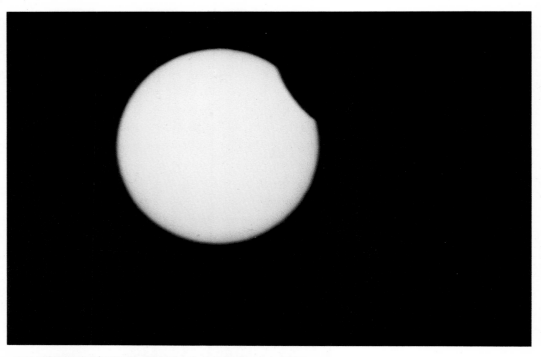

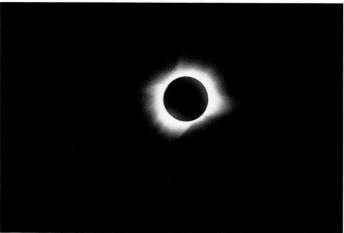

(Above) Partial eclipse of the Sun. The apparent "bite" out of the Sun is due to the encroaching disk of the Moon.
(Left) Total eclipse of the Sun, as I photographed it from Java in 1983. The dark disk of the Moon is surrounded by the corona—the Sun's outer atmosphere. The sky became so dark during the brief minutes of totality that bright stars and planets could be seen.

available accounts the opposing armies were so demoralized when the Sun began to disappear that they stopped fighting immediately, and concluded a hasty peace.

Thales was born in or about 624 BC. There is evidence that he spent some time in Egypt, and picked up what he could from the astronomers there. Though the Egyptians were accurate surveyors they were not theorists—they believed that Egypt lay in the middle of a flat Earth, and that the sky

was formed by the body of a goddess with the rather appropriate name of Nut—and in some ways Thales himself did little better. He assumed that the Earth floated in a vast ocean, and was shaped like a log or cylinder. Water was the most important of all substances, earth being produced by the condensation of water, air from rarefied water, and fire from heated water.

The only other well-known anecdote about Thales is that on one occasion he was walking

along, looking upward at the stars, and failed to notice a deep well in front of him, so that he duly fell into it. I tend to be sceptical—but after all, who knows?

Thales died around 547 BC. He was followed by various other philosophers, notably Anaxagoras of Clazomenae, who was banished from his home in Athens because of his "impiety" in teaching that the Sun was a red-hot stone larger than the Peloponnesus. Later we come to Aristarchus of Samos, who must have been a remarkably far-sighted man who went much further than Thales had dreamed of doing.

ARISTARCHUS
THE BIRTH OF COSMOLOGY

In passing straight on to Aristarchus, I may well lay myself open to criticism for saying nothing about Aristotle, who was undoubtedly one of the greatest philosophers of Ancient Greece and whose views were regarded as sacrosanct for centuries after his death. Not that Aristotle failed to make any major contributions to astronomy; he made plenty, but his basic ideas were wrong, while those of Aristarchus turned out to be right. It was Aristarchus who was bold enough to suggest that instead of being the centre of the entire universe, the Earth is in motion round the Sun.

Whether Aristarchus was the first to advance this opinion is not certain. At any rate he was one of the first, and he did his best to produce scientific evidence in support. Unfortunately most of his original writings have been lost, and have come down to us only second-hand, which is always an invitation to misunderstanding. Still, we do have his own book *On the Sizes and Distances of the Sun and Moon,* in which he made several definite statements. He maintained that the Moon shines by reflected sunlight; that the Sun is between eighteen and twenty times as far away as the Moon, and that the Sun is much the larger of the two. He also taught that the Sun may even be larger than the Earth, thereby going further than Anaxagoras had done.

His reasoning was backed up by what he took to be firm evidence. If the Moon shines by reflected sunlight, then the position at half-moon must be as shown in the diagram; a right-angled triangle, the right angle being in the position of the Moon. If one of the other angles can be found, the whole triangle can be drawn to scale. Aristarchus measured the angle at the

SUN

87°

90°

MOON　　　**EARTH**

(Above) Aristarchus measurement of Sun/Moon Ratio.
(Right) Apollo photograph of the lunar crater Aristarchus.

Earth (E) at the moment of half-moon, and found it to be 87°. It followed that the angle at the Sun (S) was 3°.

He was, of course, widely wrong; the Sun is 400 times as far away as the Moon. The angle at S is only about 10

minutes of arc, so that the angle at the Earth is over 89°. Aristarchus' principle was sound enough; it was his practical measurements which led to the error. It was not really his fault, because the Moon has a rough, uneven surface—some of its mountains rival our Everest—and so the "terminator", or dividing line between the day and night hemispheres, is certainly not smooth, making it almost impossible to judge when the phase is exactly half.

However, Aristarchus is remembered chiefly for his contention that the Earth is in motion round the Sun. This was revolutionary, and Aristarchus found few converts, because he could give no cast-iron proof that the Earth is moving; it was so much simpler to assume that it was the entire sky which was revolving, and the "Sun-centred" theory gave no better results than the old ideas had done. The other problem, of course, was religious. The era of fierce Church persecution lay in the future, but there had already been a hint of it in the case of Anaxagoras, and there seem to have been rumbles of discontent aimed at Aristarchus himself.

How did Aristarchus react? We do not know; our ignorance of his personality is complete. But at least we know now that he was correct, and in this he was centuries ahead of his time.

9

PTOLEMY
THE PRINCE OF ASTRONOMERS

(Left) Impression of Ptolemy—
though whether or not it is a good
likeness we cannot tell.

Claudius Ptolemaeus, always known to us as Ptolemy, is the last character in our story about whose character we know nothing definite. Later Arab sources say that he lived to the age of seventy-eight, and that he was a man of distinguished appearance, which is logical enough. He was born in the Greek city of Ptolemais Hermii, so that he was presumably Greek by blood; he spent all his active life in Alexandria, and was active between the years AD127 and 141 (all our dates from now on are AD). He probably died about 180, about the same time as the last of the great Roman emperors, Marcus Aurelius.

We owe Ptolemy a tremendous debt, because if it were not for his writings we would know far less about ancient science than we actually do. Strangely, later historians have been unkind to him. There have been suggestions that he was a copyist at best, and at worst a charlatan who fudged his results to make them agree with observation. Yet when the evidence is examined impartially, these slurs seem to be quite unfounded. Ptolemy was a first-rate astronomer, geographer and much else. For example, he was the first to draw a map of the civilized world which was based upon astronomical observation, and on the whole it was a good effort.

Ptolemy's major book was called the *Megale Syntaxis*, or Great Collection. It was nothing more nor less than a summary of all the scientific knowledge obtained up to that time, and it was skilfully and carefully compiled. Unfortunately the original has been lost, but it was translated into Arabic in the 9th century, so that we know it by its Arab title of the *Almagest*. It is divided into thirteen books. It includes a star catalogue, based on that of Hipparchus but with many additions by Ptolemy himself, and it also contains a full description of the then-accepted theory of the universe, which Ptolemy brought to its highest degree of perfection.

Ptolemy had no faith in the idea that the Earth might move round the Sun, and neither did he believe that the Earth spins on its axis—because if so, then clouds could never travel eastward; the Earth would outpace them. Moreover, like all his contemporaries, he believed that all celestial orbits must be circular, because the circle is the perfect form, and nothing short of perfection can be allowed in the heavens. (This obsession with circular orbits persisted right through to the time of Kepler, in the 17th century.) Yet Ptolemy, who was an excellent observer, knew quite well that the planets cannot move round the Earth in circular orbits at a constant rate. If they did, their movements against the starry background would be completely regular, which is emphatically not true. Consider, for instance, Mars. It is at its brightest every other year, and there are times when it halts its usual eastward movement against the stars, backtracks or "retrogrades" for a while, stops again, and resumes its eastward march. How could this be reconciled with observation?

Ptolemy had the answer—or thought he had. He maintained that a planet moves in a small circle or epicycle, the centre of which — the deferent — itself moves round the Earth in a perfect circle. As more and more irregularities came to light, more and more epicycles had to be introduced, and the final picture was painfully clumsy and artificial, bit it did fit the observations—and, of course, Ptolemy could know nothing about the nature of what we now call gravitation.

The real situation is very different. The Earth moves in a smaller orbit than Mars, and travels more quickly; as it "passes" Mars, the overall effect is to make the planet backtrack. This seems simple enough today, but it was far from simple to Ptolemy, and it

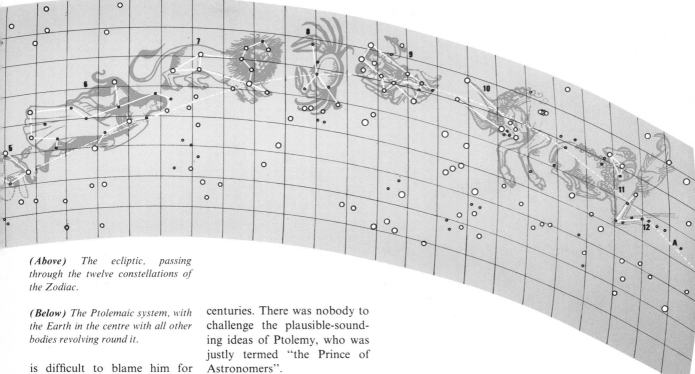

(Above) The ecliptic, passing through the twelve constellations of the Zodiac.

(Below) The Ptolemaic system, with the Earth in the centre with all other bodies revolving round it.

is difficult to blame him for being misled.

Ptolemy left us a list of forty-eight constellations, named mainly after mythological characters such as Orion, Hercules and Perseus. All these "originals" are still to be found on our maps, though in some cases the boundaries have been drastically altered. The far southern stars, never visible from Alexandria, were divided up later, so that some of the southern constellations have decidedly modern-sounding names such as the Microscope, the Telescope and the Octant.

With Ptolemy, we come to the end of an era. The Earth was regarded as supreme; astronomy was still equated with the pseudo-science of astrology, and there was no real conception of the nature of the universe. On the other hand a great deal had been learned, and we must on no account under-estimate the achievements of the Greeks, so admirably summarized by Ptolemy. With his death, the Dark Ages descended upon science; progress came to a halt, and was not resumed for many centuries. There was nobody to challenge the plausible-sounding ideas of Ptolemy, who was justly termed "the Prince of Astronomers".

ULUGH BEIGH
ASTRONOMY AND ASTROLOGY

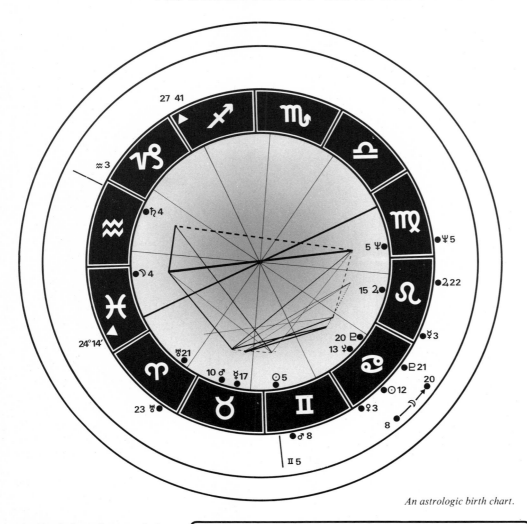

An astrologic birth chart.

Glyphs of the Signs

♈ Aries	♎ Libra		
♉ Taurus	♏ Scorpio		
♊ Gemini	♐ Sagittarius		
♋ Cancer	♑ Capricorn		
♌ Leo	♒ Aquarius		
♍ Virgo	♓ Pisces		

Glyphs of the Planets

☉ Sun	♄ Saturn
☽ Moon	♅ Uranus
☿ Mercury	♆ Neptune
♀ Venus	♇ Pluto
♂ Mars	☊ Moon's Nodes: North
♃ Jupiter	☋ South

As the Dark Ages drew to their close, astronomy was re-born—mainly for the wrong reasons. The Arabs took the lead, because they were implicit believers in astrology, and to cast their horoscopes they needed to know the positions of the stars as well as the movements of the Sun, Moon and planets. For instance there was Al-Battani, who lived from 850 to 929 and wrote an important book, the English title of which is *The Movements of the Stars;* there was Al-Sufi, who compiled a surprisingly accurate star catalogue, and there were many others. Moreover, the works of Ptolemy and other ancient scientists were translated, and thereby preserved.

The story of Arab astronomy culminated, and also ended, with the career of Ulugh Beigh, who was born in 1303. He was the grandson of the Oriental conqueror Tamerlane, and was a very powerful man indeed. At his capital, Samarkand, he set up a fully-fledged observatory, together with an Academy of Science and a large library. By "observatory" I do not, of course, mean anything in the modern sense, because telescopes still lay in the future; the main instruments were quad-rants, which were used to measure the relative positions of the celestial bodies and were reasonably accurate when used by skilful observers—as the Arabs undoubtedly were.

We know a reasonable amount about Ulugh Beigh himself. At an early age he was made Governor of parts of his father's realm, and showed himself to be a scholar of high quality; apart from his astronomy he was deeply inter-ested in Chinese art and decor-ation, even going so far as to import Chinese artists. He was an expert in studies of the Koran, and wrote poetry as well as a history of the admittedly rather dubious careers of the four sons of the famous (or notorious) Genghis Khan. He was himself a good mathemat-ician, and commissioned a book of tables of the planetary motions which was an improve-ment upon anything previously drawn up, though, predictably, he continued to regard the Earth as the centre of the universe.

Ulugh Beigh was a highly intelligent man. Unfortunately, being a scholar does not auto-matically bestow an ability to govern, and this is where Ulugh Beigh fell down. It is permissible to believe that he was more interested in art and science than in statecraft, and when managing a large and turbulent realm this will not do at all. Worse, he was a firm believer in astrology. He had a horoscope cast for his eldest son, Abdall-atif, and learned to his dismay that the boy was destined to kill him. Without delay he exiled his son, and told him firmly never to come back. Abdallatif was not to be cast aside. He raised an army, invaded his father's country, and had Ulugh Beigh murdered. That was one astro-logical prediction which came true, and it also marked the vir-tual end of the Arab school of astronomy. The date of Ulugh Beigh's death has been given as 27 October 1449.

Under the circumstances, it is not surprising that the new ruler failed to continue his father's scholarly pursuits, and no more observations came from Samar-kand. However, the real awak-ening was at hand. It came not from Arab countries, but from Europe; the stage was being set for the greatest of all revolu-tions in scientific thought.

COPERNICUS
THE GREAT REVOLUTION

Mikołaj Kopernik, always known by his Latinized name of Copernicus, was born at Toruń, in Poland, in 1473. His father was a merchant, and by the standards of the time well-off. His mother was the daughter of a very powerful politician named Łukasaz Watzenrode, who subsequently became a bishop and had a tremendous influence upon Copernicus' life.

With his brother, Nicolaus Copernicus went to the University of Cracow, and then to Bologna, where he studied canon law. He also became acquainted with a professor named Domenico Novara, and it is likely that he then had his first serious doubts about the truth of the Ptolemaic theory of a central Earth.

By 1500 he had been made Canon of Warmia, a part of Poland where Uncle Łukasz was now the local bishop. In 1501 he returned to his native country to become installed in the cathedral in Frombork, a remote region of Warmia, and became active in politics and in administration as well as in his religious duties. He was also known as a medical man, giving remedies which I would personally hesitate to try. For instance, if you want a cure for all illnesses:

"Take two ounces of Armenian clay, a half ounce of cinnamon, two drachms of tormentil root, dittany, red sandalwood, a drachm of ivory and iron shavings, two scruples of ash and rust, one drachm each of lemon peel and pearls; add one scruple each of emerald, red hyacinth and sapphire; one drachm of bone from a deer's heart; sea locusts, horn of a unicorn, red coral, gold and silver foil – all one scruple each; then add half a pound of sugar, or the quantity which one usually buys for one Hungarian ducat's worth." Encouragingly, he added: "God

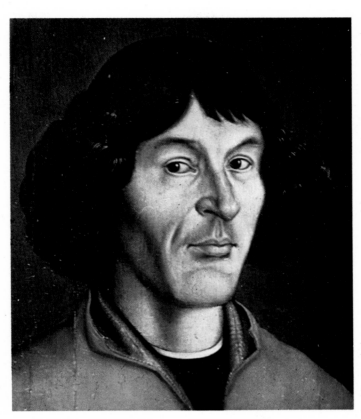

(Above) Copernicus: *anonymous portrait.*

(Below) Page from *Copernicus' great book*, De Revolutionibus Orbium Cœlestium.

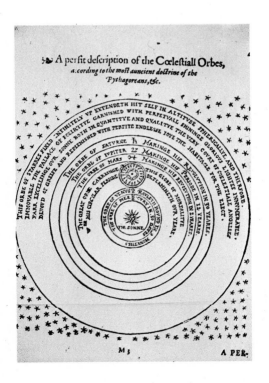

willing, it will help."

Around 1507 we know that he wrote a short book in which he stated his belief that the Earth was in motion round the Sun, but he did not have it printed; he knew, only to well, that the Church would regard such ideas as dangerously heretical—and Copernicus was himself a Church official. He had also other matters on his mind, and for a while he even had to take part in an active campaign to liberate his country from the Teutonic Knights, who had begun as a religious order but had become an unmitigated nuisance. It was 1525 before they were finally removed, and Copernicus was able to settle down to his main career.

He was more than ever convinced that the Ptolemaic theory was wrong. It was unnecessarily complicated, and Copernicus saw that most of the worst problems could be removed by replacing the Earth by the Sun in the centre of the planetary system.

His great book *De Revolutionibus Orbium Coelestium* (Concerning the Revolutions of the Celestial Orbs) was probably complete by 1533, but remained unpublished for many years, for the same reasons as before. Finally he was persuaded to let it go to press, but it appeared only as Copernicus himself lay dying in 1543.

His misgivings had been well-founded. The Church was bitterly hostile, and Martin Luther even wrote that "this fool seeks to overturn the whole art of astronomy". Moreover, it is fair to say that he fell into many of Ptolemy's errors, and was even reduced to bringing back epicycles. But he had taken the vital step, and we will never forget the quiet man from Frombork, which he had himself described as "the remotest corner of the earth".

TYCHO BRAHE
THE MASTER OF HVEN

The next main character in the story had a career which might have been taken straight out of the pages of a boys' novel. Tycho (originally Tyge) Brahe was a Dane of noble birth; his father was Governor of Helsingborg Castle, and Tycho, his eldest son, was born on 14 December 1546 at the family seat at Knudstrup, in Skaane. (To be accurate, Tycho was one of twins, but his brother died at birth.) For some reason his uncle, Jørgen Brahe, had been promised that the first-born should be handed over to him, and when Tycho's father demurred, Jørgen carried out a full-scale kidnap operation. Eventually it seems to have been amicably resolved, and the boy remained with his uncle.

Tycho was dispatched to the University of Leipzig to study law, but at an early age he was fascinated by astronomy, and nothing would deter him. The problem was solved when Uncle Jørgen plunged into a moat to rescue the King of Denmark, who had fallen in, and proceeded to die of pneumonia, leaving Tycho free to follow his natural inclinations.

From Leipzig he went to the University of Rostock, and it was here that he had part of his nose sliced off in a duel with a fellow student; he subsequently repaired the damage with "gold, silver and wax". By 1572 he was back in Denmark, and it was here that he saw something which altered the whole course of his life. A brilliant new star flared up in the constellation of Cassiopeia, and became bright enough to be seen in broad daylight. Tycho followed it carefully until it disappeared, and wrote a detailed account of it, which is why it is always known as Tycho's Star. He believed it to have astrological significance, though he did not go so far as his contemporary Georg

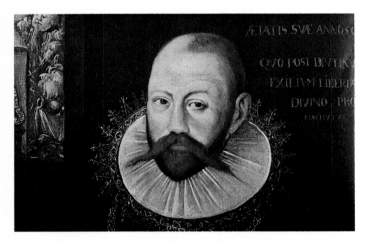

Tycho Brahe; contemporary portrait.

Busch, who claimed that the star was "formed by the ascension from Earth of human sins and wickedness . . . This poisonous stuff falls down upon people's heads, and causes all kinds of unpleasant phenomena, such as diseases, sudden death, bad weather, and Frenchmen". (What the French thought about this is not on record!)

Today we know that what Tycho saw was a supernova, involving the complete destruction of a star in a cataclysmic explosion. Since then only one supernova has been seen in our Galaxy (Kepler's Star of 1604), though we have observed many in external star-systems many millions of light-years away.

Tycho's mind was made up. An astronomer he would be, and he would have no hesitation in publishing his work, even though it had been suggested that it would be beneath the dignity of a Danish nobleman to write a book. In 1576 King Frederik of Denmark provided him with the site for a full-scale observatory, together with ample funds to maintain it. The chosen site was Hven, a small island in the Baltic between Denmark and Sweden, which suited Tycho very well. Here he

built his great "Castle of the Heavens", Uraniborg, equipping it with the best instruments which could be made at the time—mainly quadrants. Tycho was a superb observer, and between 1576 and 1596 he produced a star catalogue, which was far better than any of its predecessors, together with accurate measurements of the position of the planets. In 1577 he observed a bright comet, and proved that it was very much further away than the Moon.

Uraniborg became very much of a scientific centre, and visitors from all over the world came there (including King James of Scotland, later James I of England). No doubt the visitors were fascinated by the psychic dwarf Jep, who was always in attendance at dinnertime! Unfortunately there were problems ahead, due entirely to Tycho's own character. As well as being the virtual owner of the island, he was also its landlord, and to say that he was disliked is to put it mildly; he even added a prison to hold tenants who were slow in paying their rents. The situation became more and more strained, and after King Frederik died all funds were cut off. Finally he decided to leave, and the last observation from

Hven is dated 15 March 1596. It was in fact the last observation made there by anybody, because Uraniborg was simply abandoned, and fell down. There is nothing left of it now; when I went there a few years ago the site was marked by nothing more than a grassy plot, though there is a massive statue of Tycho close by seeming to cast a spell over the whole place.

From Denmark, Tycho went to Prague, to become Imperial Mathematician to the Holy Roman Emperor, Rudolph II, who was an abject failure as a ruler but was deeply interested in astrology—the next best thing to astronomy so far as Tycho was concerned. At Prague he continued his work, and one very important step he took was to engage a young German, Johannes Kepler, as his assistant.

Tycho may have been a magnificent observer, but as a theorist he was less successful, and though he knew that the old Ptolemaic theory was untenable he could not bring himself to believe that the Earth was anything but the centre of the universe. He followed a hybrid system, so that the planets moved round the Sun while the Sun moved round the Earth. He hoped that his studies of the planetary movement would prove him right. Ironically, the reverse happened. Tycho died suddenly in 1601, and his observations came into the possession of Kepler, who used them well—but not with the result that Tycho had hoped.

Hasty, bombastic and cruel though he was, Tycho was by far the best observer of pre-telescopic times. It is sad that he died when he did; he missed the telescope by less than a decade—and he, of all people, would have made superb use of it. Fate can sometimes by very unkind.

Tycho and his mural quadrant at Uraniborg; other instruments are also shown, with the alchemical equipment in the basement. From Tycho's Astronomicæ Instaurata Mechanica, *1587.*

JOHANNES KEPLER
THE SUN SUPREME

In most cases an astronomer, or anyone else, can be put into a definite historical period. Johannes Kepler is an exception. I have always regarded him as an "in-between" man; in many ways he was far ahead of his time, while in others he was deeply rooted in his past.

His background could not have been more different from Tycho's. He was born in 1571 at Weil der Stadt in Württemberg; his father was shiftless and irresponsible, and finally disappeared, while his mother had occult leanings and must have looked exactly like a witch. In fact, at a later stage she was

(Right) Portrait of Johannes Kepler.
(Below) Kepler's Laws.
(1) A planetary orbit is an ellipse.
(2) The radius vector sweeps out equal areas in equal times.
(3) The revolution period is linked to the distance in a definite relationship.

KEPPLERI quæ nomen habet, cur peccat imago?
Quæ tanto errori caussa subesse potest?
Scilicet est TERRÆ, KEPPLERI regula, CVRSVS:
Per vim sic sculptoris traxerat erro manum. Ob.1630.
Terra utinam nunquam currat, semperq̃ quiescat:
Quò sic KEPPLERI peccet imago minùs.
1640. Th. Lauf.

actually accused of witchcraft, and Johannes had a great deal of trouble in securing her acquittal.

However, Frau Kepler did one good deed. In 1577 she took her son outdoors to show him a bright comet (the one which Tycho saw), and from that moment on the boy was enthralled by astronomy.

In 1589 he arrived at the University of Tübingen to study theology. It was here that he became a convinced Copernican, and he was quite open about his views. In 1596 he wrote a book which contained some good ideas, plus a great deal of fantasy; for example he believed that each planet must have a "sphere" or band in space in which it was always to be found, and that these must touch each other, so that they could be linked with the five regular solids of geometry! Fortunately Tycho, in Prague, read the book and liked it. He invited Kepler to join him, and Kepler did so. On Tycho's death Kepler replaced him as Imperial Mathematician, and inherited all the Hven observations, though not without opposition from some of Tycho's family.

Kepler set out to give a final solution of the problem of the planetary motions. He had total faith in Tycho's observations, but for a long time he could not make the positions of the planets fit in with any theory. Finally he realized the truth. The planets do indeed move around the Sun—but they do so not in circles, but in ellipses. From this he was led on to draw up his three Laws of Planetary Motion, which are as follows:

1. A planet moves round the Sun in an elliptical orbit. The Sun occupies one focus of the

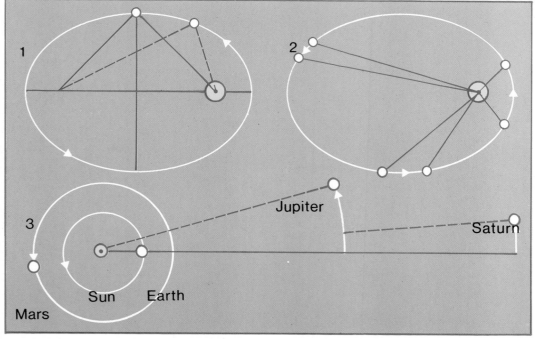

1

2

3

Jupiter

Saturn

Sun   Earth

Mars

ellipse, while the other focus is empty.

2. The radius vector—the imaginary line joining the centre of the planet to the centre of the Sun—sweeps out equal areas in equal times. (This means that a planet, or for that matter a comet, moves fastest when closest to the Sun, and slowest when furthest away.)

3. The cubes of the mean distances of the planets of the Sun are proportional to the squares of their revolution periods (so that if you know the period, which is easy to find by observation, you can also find the distance compared with that of the Earth. A complete model of the Solar System can be drawn up, and if one absolute value is known all the rest will follow.)

The first two Laws were published in 1609, and the third in 1618 in a book called *Harmony of the World,* which was the usual mixture of brilliant science and outdated mysticism. Kepler also prepared a new set of planetary tables, which appeared in 1628—long after the Emperor Rudolph had been deposed, but which Kepler dutifully called the Rudolphine Tables.

His private life had never been happy. From Bohemia he went to Linz in Austria, but had to leave there also because he was a Protestant, and Protestants were coming under increasing pressure. His final migration was to Silesia; he died in 1630 while on a journey to try to collect some of the overdue salary owed to him. His final book, a novel—the *Somnium* or Dream, about a journey to the Moon—was published posthumously.

Above all, Kepler himself was a dreamer with one foot in the ancient world and the other in the modern. Without him, the later task of Isaac Newton would have been much more difficult.

Frontispiece of the Rudolphine Tables, Kepler's last astronomical work. On the pedestal, front section, is a map of Hven, where Tycho had his observatory and made the observations upon which Kepler's Laws were based.

DEVELOPMENT OF TELESCOPES

Nobody is quite sure when the first telescopes were made. They were certainly known in Holland in 1608, and were first turned skyward shortly afterwards. Of course Galileo was the greatest of the early telescopic observers, but he was not the first. One man who preceded him was Thomas Harriott, tutor to Sir Walter Raleigh. Another pioneer was an eccentric Welsh baronet, Sir William Lower, who used a telescope to look at the Moon, and commented that the lunar face resembled a tart that his cook had made—"here some bright stuff, there some dark, and so confusedly all over".

Early refractors produced a great deal of false colour, and there were efforts to reduce this by making the focal lengths very long. In some cases the object-glass had to be fixed to a mast, and the French astronomer Auzout planned a refractor 600 feet long, though apparently it was never built. Sir Isaac Newton saw no remedy, and built the first reflector, but again he was not the originator of the idea; James Gregory had suggested it in 1663, but he had "no practical skill", as he admitted, and never tried to construct a reflector for himself.

In 1729 an English amateur, Chester More Hall, found that the way to reduce the

(Above and above right) Old meridian telescope in the Octagon Room, Old Royal Observatory (Greenwich).

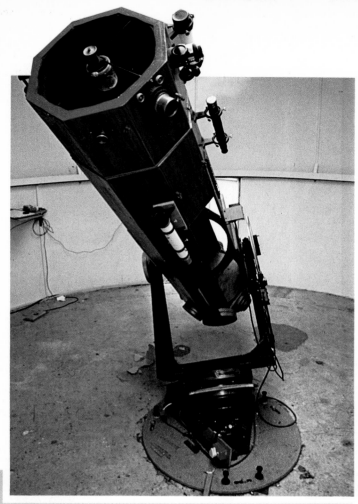

(*Left*) *An amateur telescope: my own 15-inch reflector at Selsey, in Sussex. The mounting is an equatorial fork; the telescope has an octagonal wooden tube.*

(*Above*) *Dome of the Isaac Newton Telescope at La Palma, in the Canary Islands. The telescope was originally at Herstmonceux; it has been given a new mirror and transferred to a far better site.*
(*Left*) *Dome of the Anglo-Australian 153-inch reflector at Siding Spring, Australia, as I photographed it in 1985. The site, in the Warrumbungle Mountains, is as good as any in Australia.*

false colour trouble for a refractor was to make an object-glass of two separate lenses, made of different kinds of glass. Ironically his theory was wrong, but the result was right. Hall had no wish for fame, and it was John Dollond, who rediscovered the principle in 1758 (this time with the correct theory) who is generally associated with "achromatic objectives".

Then came the large reflectors of Herschel and Lord Rosse, with their metal mirrors. But the late 19th century was the age of the great refractors, including the Yerkes and Lick giants. The Yerkes 40-inch is unlikely to be surpassed, and men such as Hale realized that the real future lay with the reflector. At the present time, Yerkes is the only major observatory where the principal telescope is a refractor.

Today there are new trends. The old, single-mirror reflectors are about to be superseded by multiple-mirror designs or by telescopes with segmented mirrors; modern computer drives mean that the equatorial mounts can be replaced by altazimuth designs; telescopes are being operated by remote control, and photography is giving way to electronic devices. Before long there will be an orbital telescope, the Hubble 94-inch reflector, and in the foreseeable future there may well be telescopes on the surface of the Moon. We have come a long way since the time when Galileo and others built their tiny "optick tubes", less than four hundred years ago.

(Above) Dome of the Russian 236-inch reflector at Mount Semirodriki, in the Caucasus. It was completed in 1976, but has never been a real success, and not many really valuable results have so far come from it.
(Left) The Yerkes 40-inch refractor, at Williams Bay in the USA. It was completed in 1897, and remains the world's largest refractor; it is in use every clear night.
(Below) Diagram of the 94-inch Hubble Telescope, due to be launched into space within the next few years.

EQUIPMENT SECT

FINE GUIDANCE OPTICAL CONTROL SENSORS (3)

AFT SHROUD

SCIENTIFIC INSTRUMENTS

AXIAL MODULES (4)

RADIAL MODULE WITH RADIATOR (1)

(Left) The AAT or Anglo-Australian telescope at Siding Spring, Coonabarabran. It has a 153-inch mirror and is completely computerized. It is not the world's largest telescope, but is arguably the best.

(Above) Dome of the UKIRT, or United Kingdom Infra-Red Telescope, on the summit of Mauna Kea. It has a thin 150-inch mirror and a lightweight mounting. It was built for infra-red, but has proved to be so good that it can also be used visually.

(Below) The Jodrell Bank 250-foot radio telescope.

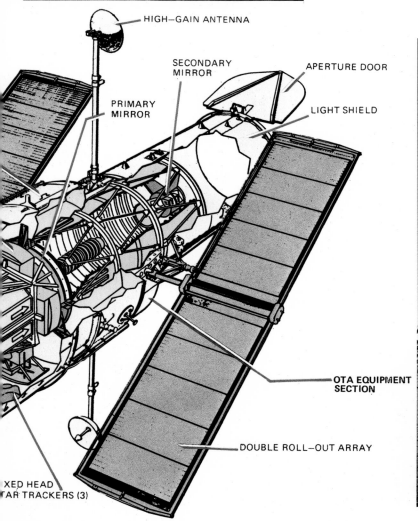

HIGH—GAIN ANTENNA

SECONDARY MIRROR

APERTURE DOOR

PRIMARY MIRROR

LIGHT SHIELD

OTA EQUIPMENT SECTION

DOUBLE ROLL—OUT ARRAY

XED HEAD
TAR TRACKERS (3)

GALILEO GALILEI
TELESCOPES AND THE STARS

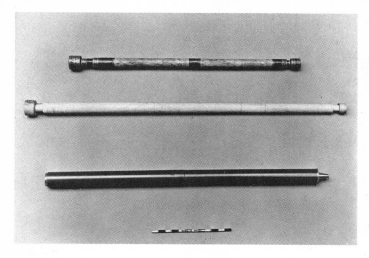

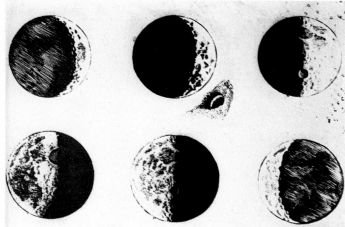

Galileo, next in our line of geniuses, was another colourful character. In its way his career was as eventful as Tycho's, even if it did not involve a kidnap or an artificial nose.

He was born in Pisa, and lived all his life in Italy, which was in some ways unfortunate. Originally he meant to study medicine, but soon changed over to science, and in 1589 he was appointed to the Chair of Mathematics at Pisa University, where his reputation spread quickly (in particular he must be regarded as the real founder of what we now call experimental mechanics, even if he never actually performed the experiment of dropping stones off the famous Leaning Tower). However, he was by no means tactful. For instance, he produced a poetic lampoon called *Against the Toga*, ridiculing the costumes of his fellow professors, and he had no respect at all for the teachings of Aristotle or Ptolemy. He also managed to offend the Governor of Leghorn, a relation of the Grand Duke of Tuscany—who had given Galileo his appointment. The Governor had designed a dredging machine for the local harbour. Galileo inspected the plans, and said bluntly that the machine would not work. It didn't; and Governor and the Grand Duke were far from pleased.

From Pisa he went to Padua,

(Above) Early Galilean telescopes. They were refractors, with single-lens object-glasses which produced an inconvenient amount of false colour; by modern standards they were low-powered, and certainly not nearly so good as present-day binoculars, but they caused a complete revolution in astronomical thought. Galileo was not the inventor of the telescope, and neither was he the first to apply it to the sky, though he was undoubtedly the first great telescopic observer.

to continue his researches; he also produced three children, though without the formality of marrying the lady concerned (later he carried on a cordial correspondence with the man she did eventually marry). By now he was a strong supporter of the Copernican system, but the real crisis began—even though he did not realize it—in 1610, when he built his first telescope.

Telescopes had been invented a year or two earlier. As soon as Galileo learned about them, he made a telescope for himself, and used it to make a series of spectacular discoveries; he saw the craters and mountains of the

(Above) Some of Galileo's sketches of the Moon. He saw the mountains and craters clearly, and by using shadow-lengths cast by the mountains he made an attempt to estimate their heights. The values which he gave for the Apennines, the most impressive of all the lunar ranges, were somewhat too great, but were at least of the right order. Galileo never drew up a complete map of the Moon, but some of the features shown in his drawings are clearly recognizable.

Moon, the four satelites of Jupiter, the changing phases of Venus, the countless stars of the Milky Way, and much else. Unlike Copernicus, he came straight out into the open. He published a book, the *Sidereal Messenger*, which showed that the telescopic revelations proved the Ptolemaic theory to be wrong.

Prudently he visited Rome, and was at first well received; he also had an ally—so he thought!—in the powerful Cardinal Maffeo Barberini. But slowly the situation worsened. Galileo was claiming that the Bible was not to be taken literally, and in the eyes of the

Church this was sheer heresy. The Holy Office (that is to say, the Inquisition) forbade him to teach Copernicanism, and for a time Galileo obeyed, but when Barberini became Pope, as Urban VIII, he felt free to speak out. In 1632 he published his great book, the *Dialogues*, which was an obvious defence of Copernicanism. Unfortunately, the Pope thought that he had been ridiculed by being presented as Simplico, one of the characters in the *Dialogues*, and from being a friend he turned abruptly into a bitter enemy. Galileo was summoned to Rome, and forced to make a hollow and perfectly meaningless recantation of the "false theory" that the Earth moves round the Sun. He had no choice but to obey, and was kept under close surveilance for the rest of his life, even after he lost his sight. He died in 1642.

It is a sorry story. The Church comes out of it very badly indeed, and Pope Urban goes down in history as a treacherous bigot. Certainly Galileo's spirit was broken, but he had at least the satisfaction of knowing that neither the Church nor any other organization could suppress the truth indefinitely. Not for another half-century would the work of Newton put a final end to the argument, but it was Galileo who together with Kepler, had made the outcome inevitable.

JOHANN BAYER
LETTERING THE STARS

After these intellectual giants, I must pause to say something about some relatively minor characters each of whom made at least one important contribution. So I next turn to a German lawyer who doubled as an amateur astronomer: Johann Bayer.

We do not know much about Bayer himself. He was born at Rhain, in Bavaria, in 1572, the year of Tycho's Star; he became an advocate in Augsburg, and died there in 1625. He never married, and about his personality our ignorance is fairly complete, though he must have had a lawyer's precise mind and command of detail. His main contribution was in allotting letters to the stars, thereby making identifications much easier. It is surprising that this had not been done before; for example the star we now call Rigel had been described by Ptolemy as "the brilliant star in the left foot of Orion", which may have been true enough but is decidedly clumsy.

In 1539 an Italian named Alessandro Piccolomini had published a set of star maps in which he gave the stars Latin letters, but it was all very vague, and Bayer preferred to use Greek. His method was straightforward enough in theory. He took each constellation, lettered its brightest star Alpha (the first letter of the Greek alphabet), the second Beta, and so on to Omega, the last Greek letter. Inevitably the system was not rigorously applied, and there are many exceptions to the rule—thus in Sagittarius, the Archer, the two leading stars are Epsilon and Sigma, with Alpha and Beta very much in the also-ran class—but it was better than nothing, and Bayer's letters are still used. Bayer also introduced some new constellations, such as Grus (the Crane) and Triangulum Australe (the Southern Triangle). His new constellations have been retained, though additions by some later astronomers have not—thus Johann Bode proposed names such as Officina Typographica (the Printing Press) and Sceptrum Brandenburgicum ("the Sceptre of Brandenburg"). Eventually, in 1932, the controlling body of world astronomy, the International Astronomical Union, took a firm line, and reduced the number of accepted constellations to eighty-eight.

Bayer's *Uranometria* became popular, and through the 17th century was more widely used than any other atlas. But perhaps unfortunately, Bayer was drawn into a venture of a different kind, which in retrospect has the air of comic relief. He became acquainted with another Augsburg amateur astronomer, Julius Schiller, about whom we know only that he was an Augustine monk. Schiller was anxious to re-name

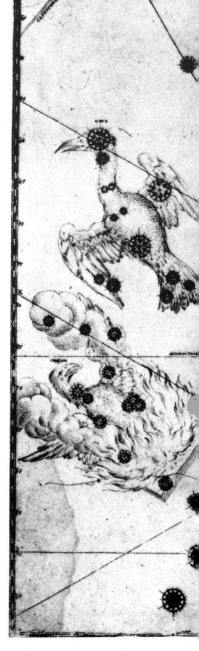

all the constellations so as to give them Christian associations. Somehow or other he persuaded Bayer to collaborate, and together with a skilful engraver they set out to alter the whole celestial scene. The Great Bear became St Peter's Boat; Cassiopeia was transformed into Mary Magdalene, Perseus

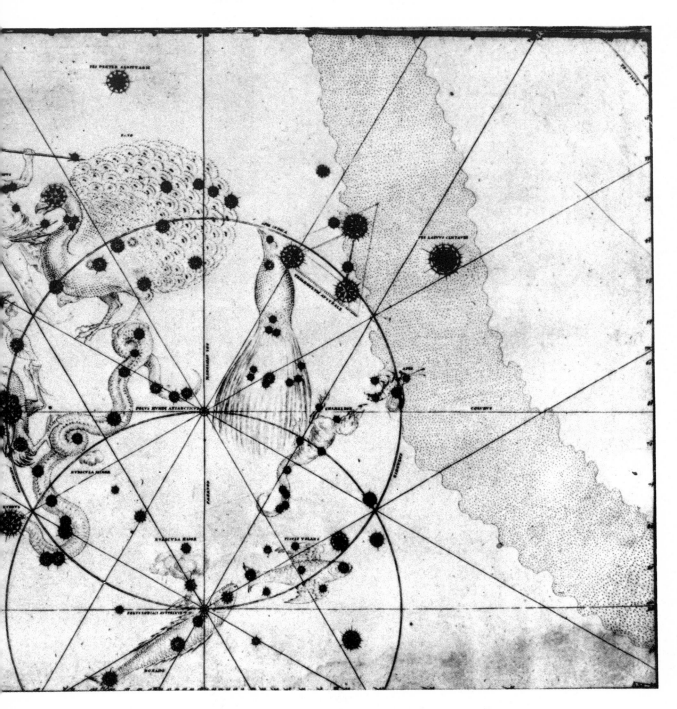

into St Paul, and so on. The Biblical figures were carefully drawn with their faces turned outward, because, Schiller was careful to explain, it would have been disrespectful to show their back sides!

Predictably, the result was a glorious muddle from the first, and moreover both of the authors died before the maps were completed—Bayer in 1625, Schiller in 1627. The manuscript was made ready for the printer by Jakob Bartsch, who had worked with Schiller and later married Kepler's daughter Susanna (he had also helped in the preparation of the Rudolphine Tables). When the maps came out, in 1627, they created no stir whatsoever.

Yet Bayer, with his legal training, had made a useful start in bringing order and method into the star-patterns, and for this he deserves to be remembered—even if we have long since forgotten St Peter's Boat!

(Above) The south polar region of the sky, also from Bayer's Atlas. Obviously this area cannot be seen from Europe.
(Far left) Map of the Serpent, from Bayer's Atlas.

JOHANNES HEVELIUS
MAPPING THE MOON

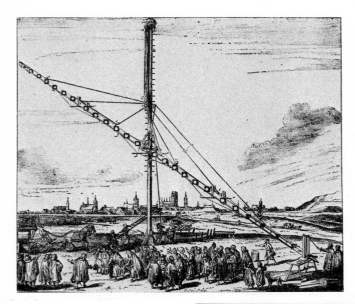

Bayer, Schiller and others busied themselves in drawing star maps. So did Johannes Hevelius, who lived in the town of Danzig—known today as Gdańsk, in Poland—and was very much involved in public life there.

He was born in January 1611, only a year after Galileo had made the pioneer telescopic observations, and was educated in Danzig, after which he spent some time in Holland and then in England (though apparently his command of the English language was always fragmentary). He was deeply interested in astronomy, and built elaborate quadrants, sundials and other instruments, including telescopes. Telescopes were a problem, because they produced an inconvenient amount of false colour, and in Hevelius' day the only remedy (and an incomplete one, at that), was to make the telescopes immensely long. One of Hevelius' telescopes had a small object-glass and a focal length of 150 feet, so that the object-glass had to be fixed to a mast. I have never understood how monstrosities of this sort could be used effectively, but Hevelius managed it.

In 1649, on the death of his father, he became the sole owner of the family brewery, and astronomy had to be restricted to his spare time, but his energy was boundless. Oddly enough, he did not use telescopic sights for his star-maps; he preferred the old-fashioned "open sights", which made some of his contemporaries very dubious about his results. Edmond Halley, then a young man building up a reputation, visited him on behalf of the Royal Society to see how he

(Left) "Aerial" telescope, of the type used by Hevelius.
(Below) Hevelius at his quadrant.

worked. Halley was always friendly and popular; he and Hevelius got on well together—though, sadly, Hevelius later took exception to some of Halley's comments, and accused him of having come to Danzig purely to spy upon him. Halley, never quick to take offence, did go so far as to describe Hevelius as a "peevish old gentleman", but there was no open quarrel.

This episode shows Hevelius up in a doubtful light, and he was clearly wrong in preferring his open sights, but he had great strength of character, as he showed when a major misfortune struck. His observatory, begun as a small room in the upper part of his house, had grown to be a large platform with two observing huts, and telescopes and instruments of all kinds, plus a magnificent library. Then, in September 1679—soon after Halley's visit—the observatory caught fire. It was totally destroyed, together with all the books and manuscripts. A lesser man would have given up. Hevelius, to his everlasting credit, did not. He rebuilt the observatory, and by 1681 it was functional again. He continued to observe until well into his seventies; he died on his 76th birthday, in 1687.

The Moon was one of his main interests, and in 1647 he produced a lunar map which was the best of his time; he also named the various features, using terrestrial analogies—thus the crater we now call "Copernicus" was his "Etna", while our "Plato" was his "Greater Black Lake". Less than a dozen of the names he gave are still in use, and neither do we have the original copperplate of his map, which was reputedly melted down after his death and made into a teapot; but his chart was a major advance, and for this alone Hevelius deserves to be remembered.

JEREMIAH HORROCKS
THE TRANSIT OF VENUS

(Left) Stained-glass window in Hoole church, honouring Horrocks. *(Right)* Carr House, from where Horrocks made his observations of the transit of Venus.

Astronomers tend to be long-lived, but there are a few cases in which careers of exceptional promise have been cut tragically short. For instance Gascoigne, inventor of the micrometer, was killed at the Battle of Marston Moor. Two others who had short but fruitful lives were John Goodricke (of whom more anon) and the Rev. Jeremiah Horrocks.

Horrocks was born in 1619. He hailed from Toxteth, near Liverpool, and went to Cambridge to study for the Anglican ministry. He was deeply interested in mathematics and astronomy, and soon began to carry out original research. He mastered Kepler's Rudolphine Tables, and was at once convinced of the truth of the Copernican theory. (He was in no danger, because at that time religious persecutions of scientists did not occur in England, though in Italy Galileo was still under house arrest.)

In checking the Rudolphine tables, Horrocks found something very interesting. There are two planets, Mercury and Venus, which are closer to the Sun than we are, so that they can sometimes pass in transit across the face of the Sun. Kepler had predicted that both Mercury and Venus would transit in 1631, and they did, though only the transit of Mercury was observed. Horrocks discovered

that there would be a transit of Venus on 24 November 1639, and he made up his mind to observe it.

He began observing on 23 November, just in case there had been an error in timing. At sunrise on the 24th he was watching again, but unfortunately it was a Sunday, and by then he had become curate in the village of Hoole, near Chester. Church services could not be postponed; Horrocks had to leave his telescope and attend to his official duties. It was not until 3.15 in the afternoon that he was able to return to observing. Then, in his own words:

"At this time an opening in the clouds, which rendered the Sun distinctly visible, seemed as if Divine Providence encouraged my aspirations when, O most gratifying spectacle! the object of so many earnest wishes, I perceived a new spot of unusual magnitude, and of a perfectly round form, that had just wholly entered upon the left limb of the Sun."

He followed the planet until sunset, an hour and a half later, and made useful measurements.

He had had time to alert only one other observer, his friend William Crabtree, who lived near Manchester. Crabtree had bad luck with the weather, but did manage to see Venus just before sunset when the clouds broke up for a few seconds.

That was the last opportunity for over a century. Transits of Venus occur in pairs, separated by eight years, with a long break between each pair; there have been transits in 1761, 1769, 1874 and 1882, while the next is due in 2004. They were once used as a means of measuring the Earth's distance from the Sun, though the method is now, of course, obsolete.

The fact that Horrocks put his clerical duties before his all-absorbing interest is a key to the firmness of his character. After all, he new quite well that there would be no more transits of Venus in his lifetime. What he could not foresee is that his life would be so short; he died suddenly on 3 January 1642.

From all accounts he observed the transit from Carr House, in Hoole. When I went there, some years ago, it had been turned into a doll museum. But Hoole has not forgotten Horrocks; a stained-glass window in the local church is a memorial to him. It is sad that he was given no time to do more.

GIOVANNI CASSINI
RINGS AND MOONS

(Above) Saturn's rings; the Cassini Division is shown.

Not all astronomers are pleasant people. Most of them are (at least, I hope so!) but there are exceptions to every rule, and it may well be that one of them was Giovanni Domenico Cassini, the next major character in our story. But first let us chronicle his achievements, which are very considerable.

He was an Italian, born in 1625. He studied at Genoa, and at the age of twenty-five was made Professor of Astronomy at the University of Bologna, where he began a series of observations with the aid of the clumsy long-focus refractors in vogue at the time. He looked at the planets, and determined the rotation periods of Mars and Jupiter with surprising accuracy (with Mars, his estimate was correct to within 3 minutes). Later he discovered the main gap in Saturn's ring system, still called Cassini's Division, and four of Saturn's satellites.

In 1669 King Louis XIV of France invited him to Paris to become first Director of the new observatory there. Cassini accepted, and never returned to Italy; he also became a French citizen, which is why he is often referred to as Jean Dominique.

In Paris he had problems to face at once. The King wanted an elaborate and magnificent building, and by the time of Cassini's arrival it was well under way. It certainly looked nice, but as an observatory it was useless, because there were awkward towers and pieces of masonry which hid much of the sky. Cassini was not pleased, but there was little he could do about it, even when part of the building started to fall down. However, he did his best.

One problem which he tackled was that of the parallax of Mars. He observed the planet from Paris, while an assistant, Jean Richer, was dispatched to Cayenne in French Guiana to observe from there. From the combined results, Cassini derived a value for the distance between the Earth and the Sun; he gave 85,700,000 miles, which was much better than any previous estimate. Sadly, Richer's subsequent career was blighted. He had achieved fame, and the jealous Cassini did not approve. He therefore sent his assistant to a remote province to work on military fortifications, and Richer was never able to contribute further to astronomical science.

Cassini was equally unpleasant to another assistant, the Danish astronomer Ole Rømer, who arrived in Paris in 1673. Rømer found conditions at the observatory far from ideal (it is said that one member of the staff was even reduced to sleeping on a windowsill), but he was not discouraged, and from his observations of the movements of the satellites of Jupiter he worked out a good value for the speed of light. Cassini refused to accept these results, but Rømer stood his ground, and was no doubt glad to leave Paris and return to Denmark—which he did in 1681—to carry out other important researches of which no doubt Cassini disapproved.

Remarkably, Cassini never accepted the Copernican theory. He was ultra-conservative as well as jealous and mean—it was curious that the premier observer of the day was so firmly rooted in the past—and remained so until his death in 1712, when he was succeeded as director by his son. Yet nothing can detract from the value of his observations, and we must remember him as kindly as possible.

CHRISTIAAN HUYGENS
TELESCOPES, CLOCKS AND LIGHT-WAVES

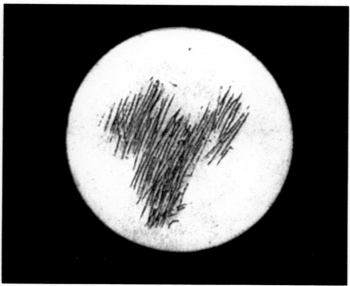

(**Left**) Christiaan Huygens; contemporary portrait.

(**Above**) Drawing of Mars made by Huygens in 1659. The V-shaped feature is the Syrtis Major, which is easily recognizable even though its size has been exaggerated. This was the first sketch of Mars which showed surface details unmistakably.

aaaaaaa cccc d eeeee g h iiiiiii llll mm nnnnnnnnnn oooo pp q rr s ttttt uuuuu . . .

Have you any idea what that means? It was an anagram published in 1656 by the Dutch astronomer Christiaan Huygens. Rearranged, it reads "Annulo cingitur, tenui, plano, nusquam cohærente, ad eclipticam inclinato"—or, in English, "Saturn is surrounded by a slender flat ring inclined to the ecliptic, but which nowhere touches the globe".

Huygens had discovered the rings of Saturn, or, rather, had realized what they were. In 1610 Galileo had seen something odd about Saturn's shape, but his telescope was too imperfect for him to decide what it was. Huygens, however, had hit on a new method of grinding and polishing lenses, and his telescopes

were far better than Galileo's. In 1656 he had also discovered Titan, the largest of Saturn's satellites.

Huygens had been born at The Hague in 1629, and soon made his mark, but his revelations about Saturn's ring system aroused a curious amount of hostility—to which Huygens replied with great modesty and restraint. Another of his contributions was the first drawing of Mars to show any surface detail. In 1659 he recorded the V-shaped feature we now know as the Syrtis Major, now known to be a lofty plateau with craters on it; it looks dark because winds have blown away the red dust so common on Mars, leaving the ground below exposed.

Quite apart from telescopic work, Huygens busied himself with something quite different:

clocks. He even invented the pendulum clock, and did his best to test it on a sea-voyage, because at that time there was no reliable timekeeper which could be used by sailors for the purpose of finding their longitude when they were out of sight of land. Unfortunately the test was not a success. Of the two clocks he took one refused to work, the other broke down as soon as the sea became rough, and Huygens' assistant was violently sick!

In 1665 Louis XIV invited Huygens to France, and Huygens went to Paris, where he stayed for the next 15 years. When he returned to Holland in 1681 (partly because he was a Protestant, and France was strongly Catholic) he spent his time mainly in making lenses of long focal length. One of them,

with a focal length of 210 feet, is now in the possession of the Royal Society. He also developed an improved type of eyepiece, still called the Huygenian. But it was his work on the nature of light which is usually regarded as his main contribution to science. Unlike Newton, he believed light to be a wave motion, and his book *Traité de la Lumière*, published in 1678, was a fundamental advance.

Huygens did meet Newton in England, but he was slow to accept the idea of Newtonian gravitation. He believed only in things which could be explained mechanically; anything else was too much like magic! But he was as good an observer as many astronomer of his time; his improvements to the telescope were invaluable—and we still use his pendulum clocks.

ISAAC NEWTON
THE LAWS OF GRAVITATION

It is often said that Isaac Newton was the greatest mathematical genius of all time. This may well be true, and there is no doubt that his work laid the foundations of all modern-type astronomy. He was born in 1642, the year that Galileo died; he died in 1727, by which time he had received every scientific honour that the world could bestow. His main contributions were made when he was comparatively young, culminating in 1687 with the publication of the immortal *Principia*, but it is quite wrong to claim—as some writers have done—that he never did anything much after 1687, and even more absurd to suggest that after a fit of depression he became mentally ill. Another piece of fiction concerns his dog, Diamond. The story goes that the dog upset some vital papers and tipped them into the fire, leaving Newton to cry out "Diamond, Diamond, you little know what you have done!" Actually Newton never kept a pet; Diamond did not exist, and neither did the precious papers.

On the other hand, the story that he watched an apple fall from a tree, and was led on to reason that the force pulling on the apple was the same as the force acting on the Moon, is almost certainly true. The apple-tree in the garden of Newton's old home at Woolsthorpe, in Lincolnshire, is still there.

Newton was a sickly child; his father died before he was born, and when his mother remarried young Isaac was brought up by his grandmother. He was of an inventive turn of mind. Initially he was far from distinguished at school, and there is yet another story (true?) that when he was mocked by a bigger boy, he determined to work hard enough to reach the top of the class, which he duly did. After a mercifully unsuccessful attempt

to turn him into a farmer, he went to Trinity College, Cambridge, to read for his degree.

At this point he came under the influence of the Lucasian Professor of Mathematics, Isaac Barrow, who was as renowned for his learning as well as for his

Replica of Newton's first reflector, presented to the Royal Society in 1671.

physical strength (he was once involved in a shipboard fight against pirates off the coast of Turkey!). Barrow recognized Newton's ability, and all was going well when the Plague struck. Cambridge University was closed, and Newton went

back to Lincolnshire. It was here, during 1665 and 1666, that he laid the foundations of his greatest work. As well as his thoughts about gravitation, he concentrated upon the nature of light, and this led on to his construction of the first reflecting telescope, which was presented to the Royal Society some years later.

When the Plague danger was over, Newton returned to Cambridge, and in 1669 Barrow resigned his Chair of Mathematics so that Newton could succeed him. Two years later Newton became a Fellow of the Royal Society, but unfortunately not everything was plain sailing; in particular Newton crossed swords with Robert Hooke, who was a brilliant researcher but who had an almost uncanny ability to upset people. Newton was over-sensitive and was never an easy man to know, which led to some bitter exchanges.

In 1684 there were frequent discussions at the Royal Society about the ways in which the planets moved. Kepler had shown that their orbits were elliptical, but the full mathematical solution had not been found. Hooke could not provide it; neither could Edmond Halley. Finally, when it became clear that the answers were not forthcoming, Halley made up his mind to consult Newton, the only man who was equal to the task. When he saw Newton at Cambridge, he found that not only could Newton solve the problem, but had actually done so—and had lost his notes!

Before Halley left Cambridge he had made Newton promise to re-work the calculations. Next, Halley urged him to write the book we know as the *Principia*. It took fifteen months to complete, and has been called the greatest mental effort ever made by one man; but Halley

[12]

AXIOMATA
SIVE
LEGES MOTUS

Lex. I.

Corpus omne perseverare in statu suo quiescendi vel movendi uniformiter in directum, nisi quatenus a viribus impressis cogitur statum illum mutare.

PRojectilia perseverant in motibus suis nisi quatenus a resistentia aeris retardantur & vi gravitatis impelluntur deorsum. Trochus, cujus partes cohaerendo perpetuo retrahunt sese a motibus rectilineis, non cessat rotari nisi quatenus ab aere retardatur. Majora autem Planetarum & Cometarum corpora motus suos & progressivos & circulares in spatiis minus resistentibus factos conservant diutius.

Lex. II.

Mutationem motus proportionalem esse vi motrici impressae, & fieri secundum lineam rectam qua vis illa imprimitur.

Si vis aliqua motum quemvis generet, dupla duplum, tripla triplum generabit, sive simul & semel, sive gradatim & successive impressa fuerit. Et hic motus quoniam in eandem semper plagam cum vi generatrice determinatur, si corpus antea movebatur, motui ejus vel conspiranti additur, vel contrario subducitur, vel oblique adjicitur, & cum eo secundum utriusq; determinationem componitur.

Lex. III.

[13]
Lex. III.

Actioni contrariam semper & aequalem esse reactionem : sive corporum duorum actiones in se mutuo semper esse aequales & in partes contrarias dirigi.

Quicquid premit vel trahit alterum, tantundem ab eo premitur vel trahitur. Siquis lapidem digito premit, premitur & hujus digitus a lapide. Si equus lapidem funi alligatum trahit, retrahetur etiam & equus aequaliter in lapidem: nam funis utrinq; distentus eodem relaxandi se conatu urgebit Equum versus lapidem, ac lapidem versus equum, tantumq; impediet progressum unius quantum promovet progressum alterius. Si corpus aliquod in corpus aliud impingens, motum ejus vi sua quomodocunq; mutaverit, idem quoque vicissim in motu proprio eandem mutationem in partem contrariam vi alterius (ob aequalitatem pressionis mutuae) subibit. His actionibus aequales fiunt mutationes non velocitatum sed motuum, (scilicet in corporibus non aliunde impeditis :) Mutationes enim velocitatum, in contrarias itidem partes factae, quia motus aequaliter mutantur, sunt corporibus reciproce proportionales.

Corol. I.

Corpus viribus conjunctis diagonalem parallelogrammi eodem tempore describere, quo latera separatis.

Si corpus dato tempore, vi sola M, ferretur ab A ad B, & vi sola N, ab A ad C, compleatur parallelogrammum ABDC, & vi utraq; feretur id eodem tempore ab A ad D. Nam quoniam vis N agit secundum lineam AC ipsi B D parallelam, haec vis nihil mutabit velocitatem accedendi ad lineam illam B D a vi altera genitam. Accedet igitur corpus eodem tempore ad lineam B D sive vis N imprimatur, sive non, atq; adeo in fine illius temporis reperietur alicubi in linea illa

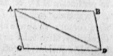

still had to use all his tact to persuade Newton to allow it to be printed, mainly because Hooke was doing his best to claim some of the credit. Eventually Halley paid for the publication out of his own pocket.

In 1689 Newton was elected a Member of Parliament, though he did not sit for very long. In 1696 he was appointed Master of the Royal Mint, and did a great deal to re-establish the coinage of the realm, which had been badly debased. He became President of the Royal Society in 1703, and remained in office until his death, though it is said that in his latter years he sometimes fell asleep during meetings. His last major book was *Opticks*, written in English rather than Latin. It was published in 1704; it had been completed some time earlier,

but Newton had decided to keep it back until after the death of Robert Hooke. He wanted no more public quarrels.

Despite all this superb work, Newton had his weaknesses. He believed in astrology (probably the last true scientist to do so) and he wasted much time in experiments on alchemy, the pseudo-science which aims to make gold out of less valuable substances. He left a mass of papers on these and similar topics, which have never been thoroughly studied because they are without value.

Newton's life was as uneventful as those of Galileo and Tycho had been turbulent, but perhaps this was just as well. Had he been forced to concern himself with more everyday affairs, we might never have had the *Principia*, the book which only Newton could write.

(*Above*) Pages from Newton's *Principia*, 1687.

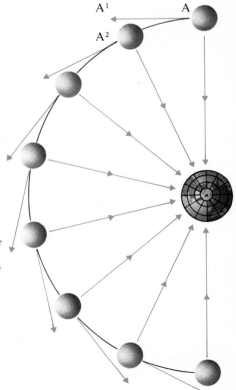

(*Right*) Newton showed that the motion of the Moon is in fact a case of accelerated motion toward the centre of the Earth. In the diagram, the Moon would move from A to A¹ if undisturbed; in fact it moves from A to A². There has therefore been a change of velocity in the direction of A¹-A² which has a component toward the Earth's centre. It is the Earth's gravitation which causes this acceleration and which keeps the Moon in orbit.

JOHN FLAMSTEED
THE ROYAL OBSERVATORY

All through the 17th century Britain's seamen were plagued by navigational problems. The main trouble was the lack of a reliable method of finding longitude. One solution, proposed in the 1670s, was to use the changing position of the Moon against the stars, because the Moon moves quickly enough to be used as a sort of cosmic clock-hand. This involved having a reliable star-catalogue, and the best one available, Tycho's, was still not good enough (Tycho, remember, had no telescopes).

The problem was taken up by a Royal Society committee, which recommended founding a new observatory for this special purpose. King Charles II was sympathetic, and ordered the construction of an observatory in Greenwich Park. The buildings were designed by Sir Christopher Wren, and the Rev. John Flamsteed was appointed Director, later assuming the title of Astronomer Royal.

Flamsteed had been born in 1646, and had graduated from Cambridge before entering the Church. He was a touchy, irritable man who suffered from chronic ill-health, but he was an expert observer, and from this point of view the choice was a good one. By July 1676 the Observatory was ready, and Flamsteed began work on the star catalogue, but his task was not easy; he had had to provide his own telescopes, and his only assistant was a "silly, surly labourer" named Cuthbert, who was much more at home in the local ale-houses than in the Observatory!

Work progressed slowly, partly because he was a perfectionist, who refused to release his results until he was completely satisfied with them. The years passed by, and still the catalogue did not appear, which led to a furious and embarrassing quarrel between Flamsteed on the one side, and Newton and Halley on the other. It was not particularly difficult to quarrel with Newton, but Halley was almost universally liked, and we have to admit that

the fault here was entirely Flamsteed's.

In 1704 Flamsteed authorized publication of the observations, though not the catalogue, and printing arrangements were put in hand. Still there were delays, and finally, in 1711, the Royal Society lost patience, producing a printed version not only of the observations, which Flamsteed had passed for publication, but also the catalogue, which he had not. Halley acted as editor, and also wrote a preface to which Flamsteed took exception.

Flamsteed did his best to revise the catalogue so that it could be re-issued, but Newton held some of the material and refused to give it back. Flamsteed was forced to re-copy the catalogue at a cost of almost £200, which did nothing to improve his temper, and when he managed to secure 300 copies of the "pirated" version he publicly burned them. In Flamsteed's eyes the chief villians were Newton and Halley, and the rift was as wide as ever when Flamsteed died in 1719. Ironically, he was succeeded as Astronomer Royal by Halley, while the catalogue was completed after his death.

At least the catalogue itself proved to be every bit as good as had been hoped. It was never used for its original purpose, because within 70 years the chronometer had been developed and made the "lunar distance" method obsolete, but the catalogue was invaluable all the same.

Flamsteed had an unattractive personality, due no doubt to his poor health, but he was totally dedicated and sincere, and he is without doubt one of Britain's greatest astronomers.

(Above) Statue of Flamsteed at Herstmonceux.
Left) The Octagon Room at the Old Royal Observatory, Greenwich.

EDMOND HALLEY

THE COMET RETURNS

Edmond Halley was born in 1656, of a good Derbyshire family. There was no shortage of money, and young Edmond went to St Paul's School, where he became Captain in 1671. Two years later he entered Queen's College, Oxford, with the promise of a brilliant career ahead. He was good-looking, good-humoured, witty and attractive. He could not have been more different from Hooke, Flamsteed or even Newton.

Before completing his degree he left Oxford and went to the island of St Helena, where he drew up the first good catalogue of the southern stars which never rise over Europe. On his return he was given an honorary degree, and made a Fellow of the Royal Society. It was due to his urging that Newton wrote the *Principia*, as we have seen; without Halley's help it would never have appeared.

For a time Halley became an official of the Royal Society (on one occasion he was given three hundred books about fishes instead of his agreed salary!) and he wrote about all sorts of subjects, ranging from the flight of birds to the date of Julius Cæsar's invasion of England, magnetic phenomena, and underwater experiments — he even made some practical tests off the Sussex coast with a

primitive diving bell. Then in 1698, he was made commander of a naval ship in order to undertake a long voyage with the aim of mapping the lines of magnetic variation. When his

Halley's Comet, photographed with the UK Schmidt telescope at Siding Spring, Australia, on 9 December 1985. The tail is well shown. Because the camera was following the comet, the stars are drawn out into short trails.

first lieutenant objected to taking orders from a "land-lubber", Halley took over the navigation himself, and brought the ship home with no trouble at all. On his second voyage, in 1699, he went as far as the Falkland Islands, where he encountered icebergs. His results were of immense value.

The quarrel with Flamsteed was sad, but perhaps inevitable. It would have been much worse if Halley had been less good-humoured. When he became Astronomer Royal he had to re-equip the observatory at Greenwich, because Flamsteed's widow had removed all the instruments, but before long he was hard at work on a long study of the movements of the Moon. The whole series took him twenty years, but he completed it successfully, and remained in office until his death in 1742.

Of course we remember Halley particularly for his work on comets; Halley's Comet was last back in 1986, and will

return once more in 2061. But he was very much of an all-rounder, and it is a pity that his reputation has been over-shadowed by Newton's.

Halley had a lively sense of humour, and was popular with almost everyone – except Flamsteed, who commented acidly that Halley "swore and drank brandy like a sea-captain". There is also a story that when the Czar of Russia, Peter the Great, came to England to learn about shipbuilding he struck up a friendship with Halley, and after a far from teetotal evening the Czar climbed into a wheelbarrow and Halley pushed him through a hedge. I have a feeling that this is true — and we do have Halley's signed receipt for two wheelbarrows . . .

In science, personalities are often unimportant, but this was not so in Halley's case. Let us remember him for all his achievements, not only for his comet. Typically, his last act before he died was to call for a glass of wine — and drink it.

JAMES BRADLEY
THE ABERRATION OF LIGHT

The first two Astronomers Royal, Flamsteed and Halley, had distinguished themselves in many ways. So did the third, James Bradley, who took over at Greenwich when Halley died. Bradley was above all a precise observer, though his greatest discovery was admittedly more or less accidental.

Bradley was born at Sherborne, in Dorset, in 1693, and went to Oxford in 1711 to study theology. He was duly ordained, and became Chaplain to the Bishop of Hereford, but his real interest was in astronomy. Through his uncle James Pound — an amateur astronomer of considerable skill — he met Halley, and the two became firm friends. In 1721 Bradley resigned his Church post to become Savilian Professor of Astronomy at Oxford, and thenceforth astronomy became his sole occupation.

At an early stage he became interested in the problem of star distances. Nobody then had any real idea of how far away the stars were; certainly they were much more remote than the Sun or the planets. The only way to find out seemed to be by the method of parallax. Cassini had used this method to measure the distance of Mars, but Mars is a near neighbour, and the parallax shifts of the stars would certainly be so small that the main hope was to observe them from opposite ends of the Earth's orbit.

In 1725 Bradley joined forces with an amateur named Molyneux, and at Molyneux' private observatory in Kew the two set out to study the star Gamma Draconis (in the Dragon), which passes directly overhead as seen from England and is thus particularly easy to measure. Over a year, they found that the star was shifting — but not in the way they had expected; it appeared to trace a

tiny circle in the sky.

According to another story which is probably true, Bradley hit upon the solution one day when he was out boating on the Thames. He noticed that when the boat altered direction, the vane on the mast-head shifted slightly even though the wind did not change. At once he realized that the same kind of effect could explain the wanderings of Gamma Draconis. The Earth is moving round the Sun, so that its direction is changing all the time; the star's light is constant. Let the Earth represent the boat, and the incoming light the wind, and the situation is clear; there is always an apparent displacement of a star toward the direction in which the Earth is moving at that moment. Bradley had discovered what we now call aberration.

(Compare, too, the effect of a walker in a rainstorm, protecting himself with an umbrella. He must always tilt the umbrella forward; otherwise he will soon be drenched.)

The real importance of the discovery of aberration was that it gave the first practical proof that the Earth really is moving round the Sun. It also shows that Bradley's measurements were remarkably accurate. Later he also found a minor, regular shift of the Earth's axis which is termed nutation.

When Bradley arrived at Greenwich, in 1742, he found that there was much to done. The whole equipment was in need of modernization, and Bradley set to work without delay. As soon as he was satisfied, he began compiling a new star catalogue. It took him many years, but the end product was a tribute to his skill. The catalogue was not only better than any of its predecessors, but incomparably better, and it is still of value today, because it helps in measuring the individual or proper motions of the stars.

The stars are so remote that they do not shift much compared with each other. Actually it had been Halley who had first shown that some stars (including Sirius) had shifted perceptibly since Greek times; Bradley was not searching for proper motions — but it is valuable to compare the measurements he made with the star positions today; and Bradley's observations were quite accurate enough for that.

Bradley died at Chalfont, in Gloucestershire, in 1762. He had been an admirable Astronomer Royal, and without doubt a worthy successor to Edmond Halley.

(Above) The Old
Royal Observatory in
Greenwich Park,
showing the time-ball.
(Right) Bradley's
zenith sector, which he
used in his attempts to
measure the parallax of
a star—in which he
failed, though his
researches did lead to
the discovery of the
aberration of light.

PROBES TO THE INNER PLANETS

There is an interesting "aside" to the two probes which by-passed Venus in June 1985. Originally, Venus was to be their only target, but at an international conference at which Russian scientists were present a French astronomer made the casual comment that it would be possible to send the two vehicles on to the rendezvous with Halley's Comet. Apparently the Russian delegates departed hastily to put forward this scheme, and it was put into operation. After the Venus rendezvous, the Vega 1 and Vega 2 space-craft did indeed go on to by-pass Halley's Comet in March 1986.

(Left) The last picture of Mercury from Mariner 10, in 1974; the equipment had started to fail, but definition is still good.
(Below) Mariner 10, the only probe to have by-passed Mercury. It is still orbiting the Sun, but all contact with it has been lost.

Apart from the Japanese and European probes to Halley's Comet, the only nations to have sent vehicles beyond the Earth-Moon system up to the present time are the United States and the Soviet Union. The first attempt was a Russian one. On 12 February 1961 Venera 1 was launched, but when it was still less than 5,000,000 miles away contact with it was lost—so that it must be classed as a failure, though it may well have by-passed Venus in the following May. The first successful planetary probe was America's Mariner 2, which passed within 21,000 miles of Venus in December 1962 and sent back our first reliable information about that decidedly unwelcoming world.

Since then Venus has been contacted on numerous occasions. The Russians have succeeded in soft-landing capsules there, and have obtained pictures direct from the surface—no mean feat in view of the intensely hostile conditions; no probe can survive for more than an hour or two. Moreover, both the Russians and the Americans have put vehicles into Venus orbit, and by now we have good maps of virtually the entire globe. We know a great deal about the plains, the valleys, and the great shield volcanoes which are almost certainly active.

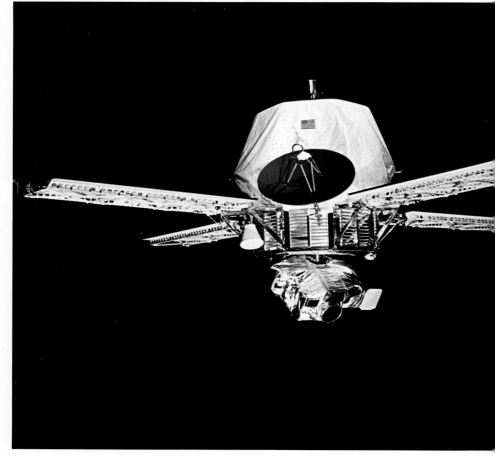

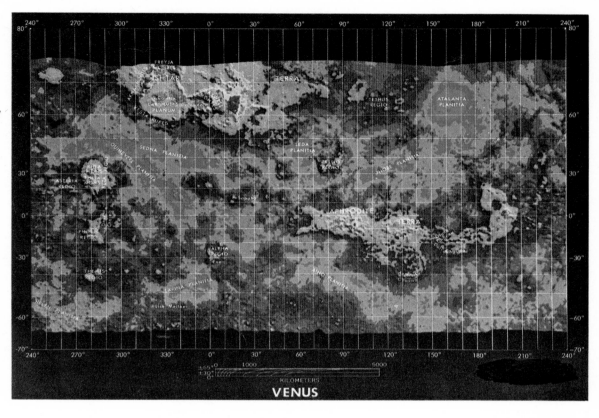

*(**Right**) Map of Venus, obtained from Pioneer 12, the probe put into orbit round the planet in 1978. This is a contour map; low-lying areas in blue, higher ones in yellow and red—it should not be mistaken for a land-and-sea map! The volcanically active regions are Beta Regio, with the shield volcanoes Rhea Mons and Theia Mons, and Atla Regio. Note the two main highland areas, Ishtar and Aphrodite, and the Maxwell Mountains, the highest peaks on Venus.*

With Mars the whole situation has been different. Mariner 4 led the way in 1964, obtaining close-range pictures which showed the presence of craters and the total absence of canals. Mariners 6 and 7 obtained better pictures in 1969, and then, in 1971, Mariner 9 went into orbit round Mars and showed the huge volcanoes there; altogether it transmitted nearly 1,400 high-quality pictures before its power failed in October 1972. Then, in 1976, came the two Viking landers, giving us our first views from the actual Martian surface.

Yet though the Russians have now launched seven probes to Mars, they have had virtually no success at all. Either their vehicles have missed the planet, or have gone out of contact, or have crash-landed. This is indeed strange; Mars should be a much easier target than Venus. No doubt fresh attempts will be made in the near future, and there are also plans for sample-and-return probes, so that before 2000 we should be able to study Martian materials in our laboratories—and give a final answer to the age-old question: "Has there ever been life on Mars?"

Mercury has so far been contacted by only one probe (Mariner 10), but here too there must surely be progress before long, and we also look forward to the first asteroid contact; the little world of Amphitrite is scheduled to be by-passed by the US Galileo probe en route to Jupiter. Already the inner part of the Solar System has been well surveyed.

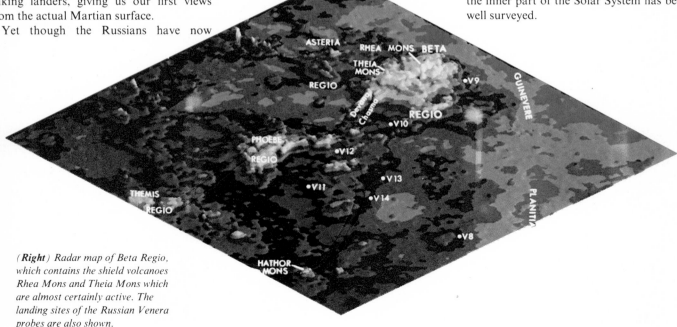

*(**Right**) Radar map of Beta Regio, which contains the shield volcanoes Rhea Mons and Theia Mons which are almost certainly active. The landing sites of the Russian Venera probes are also shown.*

37

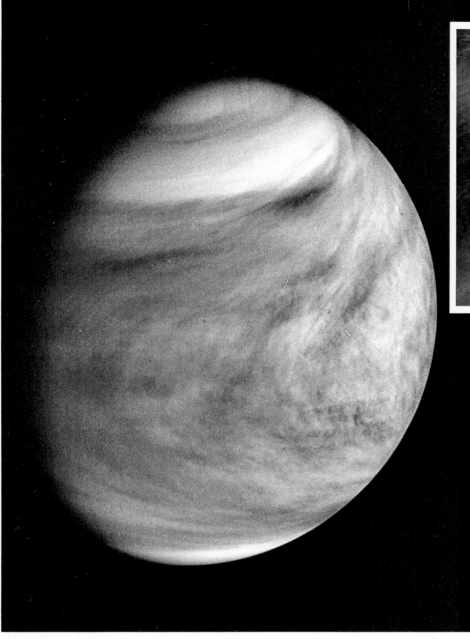

(*Far left*) *Crescent Venus, from the Pioneer orbiter. Little detail is shown; the cameras recorded the upper part of the cloud layer.*

(*Left*) *Venus, from Pioneer 12. The cloud markings are clearly shown, and also the different pattern near the planet's pole.*

(*Top right*) *The polar region of Mars, from the Viking orbiter. The white polar deposit is very obvious.*

(*Below*) *The surface of Mars, from Viking 1; the region of Chryse. The "scoop" is designed to collect Martian material and draw it into the main space-craft for analysis. The whole region is red and rock-strewn.*

MIKHAIL LOMONOSOV
THE ATMOSPHERE OF VENUS

The modern Soviet Union is one of the leading scientific nations, but things were very different in the 18th century. It was not until the career of Mikhail Lomonosov that Russian astronomy began to make real progress.

Lomonosov was born on an island off the coast of Archangel, in 1711. His father was a fisherman, and during his boyhood Mikhail went on several fishing expeditions well inside the Arctic Circle. Like most young Russians he had very little schooling, but by the time he was fifteen he knew how to read and write, and it is said that he ran away from home and joined a train of sleds carrying frozen fish to Moscow. In 1735 he gained an entrance to the University of St Petersburg, and a year later he and other students went to Marburg University in Germany to study chemistry and mining.

His career was anything but smooth. He was very far from being a teetotaller, and some of the staid German professors were deeply shocked at his behaviour, both at Marburg and at his next university, Freiburg. When he returned to Russia, in 1741, he abandoned the wife whom he had married soon after arriving in Marburg, and the situation was made even worse when he insulted one of the members of the St Petersburg Academy and served eight months in prison. It was not a promising start, but, remarkably, he was able to re-establish himself. By 1745 he was made a full member of the Academy, and was appointed Professor of Chemistry.

Whatever may be said about Lomonosov's character, there could be no doubt about his ability, and he was almost incredibly versatile. He was a pioneer of what we now call the kinetic theory of gases; he was a geologist and a meteorologist; he investigated aurora and electrical phenomena; he developed a solar furnace, using lenses and mirrors; and he was also a poet, grammarian and classical scholar. One of his best poems was written in prison!

Astronomically, his main contribution was probably his open support of the Copernican system; at that time, most Russian scientists still clung to the old idea of a central Earth. He was also a good observer, particularly well remembered for his observations of the transit of Venus in 1761. As the planet passed on to the Sun's disk, Lomonosov saw that it was surrounded by a kind of halo, and from this he correctly deduced that Venus has a dense atmosphere. We know now that the atmosphere is in fact much thicker than ours; it is made up chiefly of the heavy, unbreathable gas carbon dioxide, and the clouds contain sulphuric acid, so that Venus is not an inviting world — particularly as the surface temperature is not far short of 1000° Fahrenheit.

Lomonosov died in St Petersburg in 1765. Though he received a great many scientific honours, both inside and outside Russia, he was too outspoken to be popular, and in his later years he became more and more bitter and unsociable; but he deserves to be honourably remembered as the first great Russian astronomer.

Lomonosov's old observatory in Leningrad.

CHARLES MESSIER
THE "FERRET OF COMETS"

Now and then we come across an astronomer who makes his reputation for one line of research only. Such a man was Charles Messier, who was born in Lorraine in 1730. He came from a poor background, and his schooling was limited, but at least he had clear, neat handwriting, and this stood him in good stead when he came to Paris at the age of twenty-one to seek his fortune. He applied to Nicholas de l'Isle, Astronomer to the French Navy, who had set up a small observatory in the Hôtel de Cluny in Paris, and de l'Isle employed him—mainly as a clerk whose duties were to keep the observatory records. Messier was satisfied, because he already had a keen interest in astronomy, dating from the time when he had seen the brilliant six-tailed comet of 1744.

Then came another stroke of luck. Edmond Halley had predicted that the comet of 1682 would return in 1758, and de l'Isle instructed Messier to

(Above) The Trifid Nebula is also known as M.20—a continuing reminder of Messier's catalogue.

search for it, using a small reflecting telescope. Nothing could have suited Messier better, and at last, on 21 January 1759, he located the comet — but two major disappointments followed. First, for some strange reason, de l'Isle refused to let him announce the discovery. Secondly, he later found that he had been forestalled; Halley's Comet had been sighted by Palitzsch, in Germany, as early as Christmas Night 1758.

To his credit, Messier refused to be discouraged, and from that time on he devoted all his observing time to hunting comets. In the end he found more than a dozen, and after de

(Above) One of the brightest comets of the last decade, spotted by Bennett, a South African amateur, who followed in the tradition of Charles Messier.

l'Isle's retirement in 1760 he had more or less of a free hand. His enthusiasm was boundless— even when his wife was dying it was with great reluctance that he dragged himself away from his telescope. In 1781 he had a serious accident, falling over twenty feet into an ice-store and breaking numerous bones, but within a few months he was observing again.

One problem, he found, was that he was often misled by misty-looking patches in the sky which looked like comets, but turned out to be star-clusters or

nebulae. They wasted an incredible amount of time, and finally Messier decided to catalogue them as "objects to avoid". Ironically it is by his catalogue that he is best remembered today; we still use the M numbers—thus the Andromeda Spiral is M.31, the Orion Nebula is M.42, and so on.

Messier was no mathematician, and was quite incapable of calculating orbits for his comets; much of this work was done for him by Bouchart de Saron—an aristocrat who, sadly, was executed during the Revolution in 1794 (it is said that his last calculations were made in prison a few days before his death). It may be true to say that Messier's talent was limited, but certainly he merited the nickname bestowed on him by Louis XV of France—the "Ferret of Comets". His last discovery was made in 1798, and he continued to observe until only a few years before his death in 1817.

NEVIL MASKELYNE
CLOCKS AND ALMANACS

(Above) Nevil Maskelyne; contemporary portrait (National Maritime Museum). (Below) One of

John Harrison's chronometers, now restored to full working order and on view in the National Maritime Museum.

When James Bradley died, he was succeeded at Greenwich by Nathaniel Bliss. Bliss himself died only two years later, and was in turn succeeded by Nevil Maskelyne, who had been born in London in 1732 and had been ordained in the Church after his education first at Westminster School and then at Cambridge. Maskelyne had been Bradley's assistant, and was known to be a careful, accurate observer, so the choice was a good one.

One of his famous investigations concerned the density of the Earth. By using a plumb-line he measured the mass of a Scottish mountain, Schiehallion, and from this deduced that the Earth was, on average, between 4.6 and 4.9 denser than an equal volume of water; the real value is 5.5, so that Maskelyne was not very wide of the mark. He was also one of the first to realize that the object discovered by William Herschel in 1781 was not a comet, as Herschel had believed, but a new planet (the one we now call Uranus). But Maskelyne and Herschel did not always agree. Herschel believed the Moon and planets to be inhabited; Maskelyne was much more cautious — on one occasion he forced Herschel to modify a scientific paper before it could be passed for publication.

Maskelyne was particularly interested in the problem of longitude-finding, which still bedevilled British seamen. The method of "lunar distances", using the Moon as a clock-hand, was sound enough in theory, and Maskelyne put his faith in it, which led him on to produce a regular almanac containing all the relevant tables and navigational aids. The first issue of the *Nautical Almanac* came out in 1767, and has continued ever since, though it has now been combined with American publications. From

the outset it was found to be of the utmost value, and is probably to be regarded as Maskelyne's most important contribution.

If a really accurate time-keeper could be made, suitable for being carried on long sea voyages, the longitude problem could be solved at once. Meanwhile the Board of Longitude, set up by the British Admiralty, had offered a prize of £20,000 to be given to the first man to provide a really reliable method. In 1757 John Harrison, a skilful clockmaker, told the Board that he had completed a chronometer, and meant to apply for the award. Preliminary tests were encouraging, and in 1764, Harrison took his chronometer on a journey to the West Indies, accompanied by Maskelyne and another astronomer from Greenwich, Charles Green. The test involved working out the longitude at a selected point by traditional methods, and then comparing it with the value derived by Harrison's chronometer. The results were excellent; the timekeeper was good to a tenth of a second per day.

Yet the Board was not satisfied, and Harrison was infuriated when Maskelyne had the watch under test at Greenwich for a year and then issued an unfavourable report on it. Harrison even accused Maskelyne of deliberate dishonesty—a charge which was probably quite unfounded, even though Maskelyne was prejudiced against clockmakers and seems to have disliked Harrison personally. Harrison did receive the award in the end, though not until King George III had intervened on his behalf.

Maskelyne continued to observe, and his administration at the Royal Observatory was excellent. He remained as Astronomer Royal until his death in 1811.

WILLIAM HERSCHEL
PLANETS, STARS AND TELESCOPES

We come next to William Herschel, perhaps the greatest observer in the history of astronomy. He is best remembered for his discovery of the planet Uranus, but in fact his most important work was in

(Above) Portrait of William Herschel. (Below) Reflecting telescope made by Herschel and sent to Spain; sadly, it no longer exists. The mounting is of the same type as that used for the great 49-inch reflector.

connection with the stars.

He was born in 1738 in Hanover, then joined with Britain under one king, and was christened Friedrich Wilhelm, though we always know him as William. His father was an Army musician, and the boy joined the Hanoverian Guard, but service life did not appeal to him, and after some rather uncomfortable experiences he left hastily—though he was no deserter; he had never been formally enlisted, so that he

acted quite properly. In 1757 he arrived in England, and apart from a few visits to Hanover he spent the rest of his life there.

Herschel was an expert musician, and within a few years of his arrival in England he became organist at the Octagon Chapel in Bath, then the country's most fashionable spa. Socially he was an undoubted success; he was clever, good-looking and attractive. His sister Caroline soon joined him from Hanover, to act as his housekeeper and also to follow her own singing career, and there is little doubt that if William's attention had not been drawn to astronomy he would have ended his days as a popular and talented musician.

But astronomy had attracted him. Once installed in Bath, he looked round for a good telescope, and when he failed to find one he decided to try his hand at mirror-grinding. After many failures he produced a tolerable telescope, and began his surveys of the sky. From the garden of his home at No. 19 New King Street, Bath, he made

the discovery which was to change his whole life. On 13 March 1781 he came across an object which he knew could not be a star; he believed it to be a comet, but before long it became clear that he had found a new planet, moving round the Sun far beyond Saturn. We now call it Uranus.

King George III was genuinely enthusiastic about astronomy, and he gave Herschel a pension which made it possible for him to devote his whole time to studying the skies, keeping music as a hobby. He and Caroline moved from Bath to Slough, near Windsor Castle, and from here Herschel carried out his most extensive "surveys of the heavens", always helped by Caroline, who acted as his recorder. (Incidentally, she was herself a good observer, who discovered no less than six comets.)

Herschel's telescopes were excellent; the largest of them had a mirror 49 inches in diameter—far larger than any previously made (though, to be candid, it was unwieldy and difficult to handle). Discoveries came thick and fast. Herschel was the first to work out the approximate shape of the Galaxy; he established that many double stars are physically-associated pairs or "binaries"; he found hundreds of new star-clusters and nebulæ, and he also made observations of the planets. It is true that he had his eccentricities; he was a firm believer in the habitability of the Moon and planets, and he even thought that there could be intelligent beings living in a cool region below the surface of the Sun, but as an observer he was supreme. By the time he died, in 1822, he had achieved more than would have seemed possible for any one man.

PIERRE LAPLACE
THE BIRTH OF THE PLANETS

The nebular hypothesis, proposed by Laplace, assumed that before the birth of the planets the Solar System consisted of a gas-cloud which shrank because of gravitational forces. This resulted in an increase in the speed of rotation and a ring separated from the nebula; the ring slowly condensed into a planet. Further rings were then thrown off, each producing a planet.

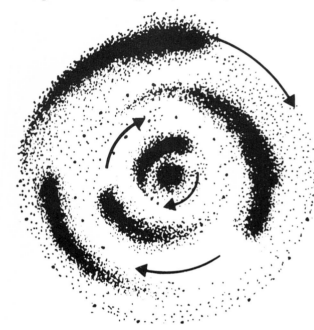

How was the Earth born? Many theories have been put forward; one of the most famous is the so-called Nebular Hypothesis, and it is for this that we best remember the Marquis de Laplace.

Laplace was born at Beaumont-en-Auge, in Normandy, in 1749. He was originally destined for the Church, but he was much more interested in mathematical science, and after attending Caen University he went to Paris with a letter of introduction to the famous mathematician Jean d'Alembert. To test him, d'Alembert set him a problem and told him to bring back the solution in a week's time. Laplace produced the answer within twenty-four hours and d'Alembert promptly offered him a position in the Military School.

He was elected to the Academy of Sciences in 1773, and his theoretical work on astronomy began at about the same time. For the next fifty years he produced a whole series of brilliant papers which were of fundamental importance in what we now call celestial dynamics. In 1796 came his book *Système du Monde,* in which the Nebular Hypothesis was proposed.

According to Laplace, the Solar System began as a rotating gas-cloud. As it shrank, under the influence of gravitation, it threw off successive rings, each of which condensed into a planet—in which case the outermost planets would be the oldest, and the inner planets, such as the Earth, considerably younger. The theory was widely accepted, and continued to be so for much of the nineteenth century, but gradually it was found to contain fatal mathematical flaws, and eventually it

was abandoned, to be replaced by theories of very different type. For example, it was suggested that the Earth and other planets were pulled off the Sun by the action of a passing star, or that the planets were born from a former companion of the Sun which exploded as a supernova.

These ideas, too, were found to be wanting, and by now we have come back to the idea of a shrinking, spinning gas-cloud, with the planets being built up by "accretion", with the Sun representing the centre of the original cloud. This is considerably different from Laplace's original picture, but the basic ideas are there. It is also notable that Laplace considered a small, dense body pulling strongly enough to prevent light from escaping from it—an almost uncanny anticipation of the Black Hole theories of today.

Quite apart from his scientific work, Laplace was very much involved in public life. When Napoleon came to power in France, in 1799, he made Laplace his Minister of the Interior, though after a few weeks he replaced him and elevated him to the Senate. Later, in 1814, Laplace voted against Napoleon and in favour of restoring the French monarchy, so that he was the target of strong criticism—the more so when he was created a marquis. He was again criticized in 1826 when he refused to support an Academy motion in favour of a free press. But it is as a master mathematician that he is remembered, and he continued his scientific work until shortly before his death on 5 March 1827.

JOHANN ELERT BODE
ASTEROIDS AND YEARBOOKS

Throughout the story of science there have been energetic popularizers, who do their best to interest those who have no official training. In astronomy the names of Sir Robert Ball, Sir James Jeans, and (today) Carl Sagan are known to most people. One of the first great popularizers was a German, Johann Elert Bode, who was born in Hamburg in 1747 and published his first treatise while still in his teens. He was a born mathematician, and a self-taught astronomer; by 1772 he was working at the Berlin Academy as editor of the *Astronmisches Jahrbuch* or Astronomical Yearbook—a post he held for half a century.

Bode revolutionized the Yearbook. It had had anything but a good reputation, but under Bode's direction it flourished, and was circulated all over the world. Not that Bode spent all his time working on it; he became Director of the Berlin Observatory in 1786, and did his best to bring the rather primitive equipment there up to date. He produced two excellent star atlases (introducing some new constellations with peculiar names, most of which have now been mercifully forgotten), and he was the first to suggest the mythological name of Uranus for the planet discovered by Herschel in 1781; Herschel himself had wanted to call it "the Georgian" in honour of his patron King George III, but not surprisingly, foreign astronomers were unimpressed.

Bode was an enthusiastic popularizer, but is probably best remembered for his connection with a curious law worked out in the 1770s by Johann Titius of Wittemberg. It concerns the distances of the planets from the Sun; because Bode made it well known it is usually—and rather unfairly—known as Bode's Law. In all probability it is due to nothing more than sheer coincidence, but it worked quite well out as far as Saturn, and when Uranus was found to fit into the scheme most astronomers jumped to the conclusion that it was really significant. It indicated that there ought to be an extra planet moving round the Sun between the orbits of Mars and Jupiter, and in 1800 six astronomers met at the private observatory belonging to Johann Schröter, near Bremen, with the intention of organizing a search for it. Clearly it would be faint, and so the self-styled "celestial police" allotted themselves different regions of the sky and set to work. Ironically, they were forestalled. On 1 January 1801—the first day of the new century—Giuseppe Piazzi, at Palermo Observatory in Sicily, found a moving object which proved to be a small planet in just the area indicated by Bode's Law. Piazzi named it Ceres, in honour of the patron goddess of Sicily. Three more "asteroids" (Pallas, Juno and Vesta) were found within the next few years, and today the total number of known asteroids is over 3,000, though most of them are very small. It has been suggested that they are the fragments of an old planet which met with disaster in the remote past, though it is more likely that they represent material "left over", so to speak, when the main planets were formed.

Neptune, discovered in 1846, does not fit in with the Law, and few modern astronomers have any faith in it. But at least Bode's work as a popularizer was a major contribution; he retired from Berlin Observatory in 1825, and died in the following year.

(Left) Camelopardalis, the Giraffe, one of the constellations introduced by Bode. It is in the far north of the sky, and contains no bright stars or definite patterns; it takes a great effort of the imagination to liken it to a giraffe or anything else!

CAMELOPARDALIS, TARANDUS AND CUSTOS MESSIUM.

HEINRICH OLBERS
WHY IS IT DARK AT NIGHT?

Dr Heinrich Olbers is one of the more attractive characters in the story of astronomy. He was a distinguished medical man, who was universally popular; as an amateur astronomer he carried out important researches, and was a source of inspiration to many of his contemporaries, including Bessel and the great mathematician Karl Gauss.

Olbers was born near Bremen on 11 October 1758. In 1777 he went to Göttingen to study medicine, but his interest in astronomy was already pronounced, and he even became director of a small observatory. He was very skilled in mathematics even at this early age, and began to compute comet orbits; later he made several discoveries—one of his comets, discovered in 1815, has a period of 70 years, and has been seen at two subsequent returns (the last being in 1956, when it almost attained naked-eye visibility).

In 1781 he received his medical degree, and began to practise in Bremen, continuing to do so until he retired in 1823. Meanwhile he had built an elaborate observatory, and became an expert observer. He was one of the "celestial police" who assembled in 1800 to hunt for the missing planet between Mars and Jupiter, he was the

*(**Above**) Heinrich Olbers, eminent doctor and amateur astronomer.*

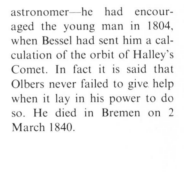

*(**Right**) Vesta, the brightest asteroid, photographed by the late F J Acfield. Ceres is indicated by the markers.*
*(**Below right**) The main asteroid belt, in the region between the orbits of Mars and Jupiter. All the first-discovered asteroids keep to this region. The ellipse shows that orbit of one of the "exceptional" asteroids. Phœthon, discovered in 1978, which is only about a mile in diameter and has a path carrying it within the orbit of Mercury. The Trojan asteroids move in the same orbit as Jupiter, and there are other exceptional objects, such as Chiron, which moves mainly between the orbits of Saturn and Uranus.*

first to recover Ceres in 1802, and he was the sole discoverer of Pallas (in 1802) and Vesta (in 1807).

In 1823 Olbers published an interesting paper in which he asked "Why is it dark at night?" He reasoned that if the universe is infinite, then sooner or later every line of sight will be covered by a star, and the sky should appear brilliant. Olbers explained the darkness by assuming that space is not transparent, so that the light from remote stars is absorbed. In fact this explanation would not fit the facts, because the

absorbing material would itself become so strongly heated that the result would be the same. The real answer is that distant objects are receding, and their light is red-shifted. Moreover, the observable universe at least does not now seem to be infinite; it may be limited at around 15,000 million light-years.

Olbers was interested in all branches of astronomy, and also in meteorological and historical matters. He contributed to all the leading periodicals of the time, and it was due to him that Friedrich Bessel decided to become a professional

astronomer—he had encouraged the young man in 1804, when Bessel had sent him a calculation of the orbit of Halley's Comet. In fact it is said that Olbers never failed to give help when it lay in his power to do so. He died in Bremen on 2 March 1840.

*(**Below**) G Piazzi, Director of the Palermo Observatory, who discovered the first asteroid, Ceres, during the compilation of a star-catalogue.*

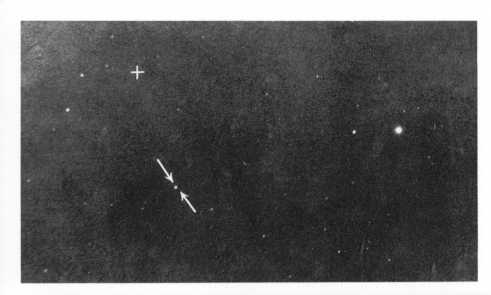

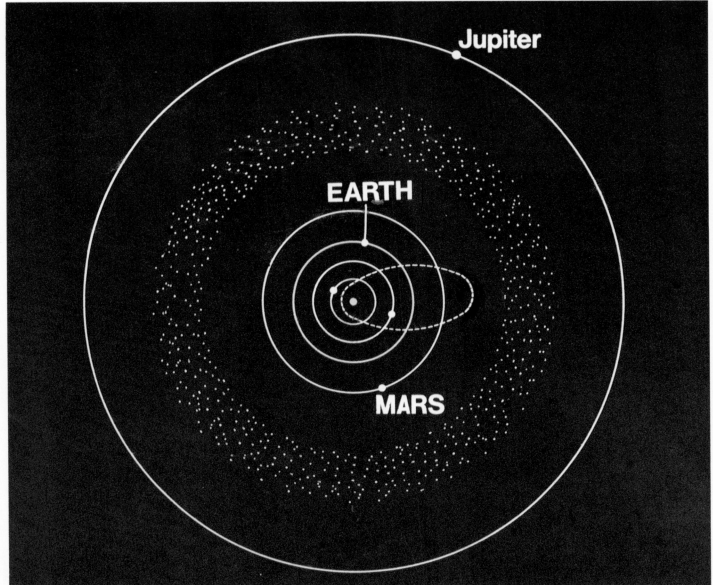

JOHN GOODRICKE
ALGOL, THE "WINKING DEMON"

If there could be a prize for the title of the most unusual astronomer in history, John Goodricke might easily be the winning candidate. He was deaf and dumb, and died at the age of twenty-one, but during his short life he made some tremendous discoveries. Lacking both hearing and speech, he showed that there was certainly nothing the matter with his brain, and he was a gifted mathematician as well as an expert observer.

He was born in Holland, at Groningen, in September 1764, but his parents were English, and he spent most of his life in York. His love of astronomy was always obvious, and he begun observing, with a particular interest in variable stars. These are exactly what the name implies: stars which change in brightness over short periods instead . of shining steadily for year after year. When Goodricke was born, only five variable stars were known. One of these was Algol, in the constellation of Perseus. Normally it is about as bright as the Pole Star, but every two and a half days it gives a long, slow "wink", taking four hours to fade down, remaining at minimum for a mere twenty minutes, and then brightening up once more, after which nothing seems to happen for another two and a half days.

In mythology, Perseus was a dashing hero who rescued the beautiful Princess Andromeda by using the head of the hideous Gorgon, Medusa, whose glance would turn any living thing to stone. Just as Andromeda was about to be gobbled up by a particularly ferocious sea-monster. Perseus petrified it, after which he duly married the princess (one of the few old legends to have a happy ending). Algol lies in the Gorgon's head, and is often known as the "Winking Demon" because of

its strange behaviour (though in fact it now seems that its variability was not known in ancient times; it was first noticed by the Italian astronomer Montanari in 1669).

Goodricke was puzzled by Algol, but finally, in 1782, he hit upon the truth. Algol is not genuinely variable at all. It is made up of two stars, one brighter than the other, revolving round their common centre of gravity in a period of two and a half days. When the fainter member of the pair passes in front of the brighter, some of the light we receive is cut off, and Algol winks. Stars of this kind are known as eclipsing binaries; Goodricke soon found another, Beta Lyrae, which lies close to the brilliant Vega.

Goodricke next discovered a third variable, Delta Cephei in the far north of the sky. This time the behaviour was different. Delta Cephei did not wink; it varied all the time, taking 5.3 days to pass from one maximum to the next. Goodricke claimed that this was a true variable, not an eclipsing binary, and again he was right. The star has given its name to a whole class of important variables, the Cepheids.

By now Goodricke was in touch with many astronomers all over the world; but, like Horrocks, he was given no time to build upon his brilliant start, and he died suddenly in York on 20 April 1786. Yet his home city has not forgotten him; there is today a Goodricke Society whose aim is to a help those people unfortunate enough to be born deaf and dumb.

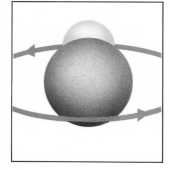

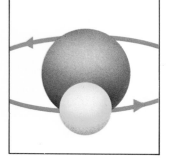

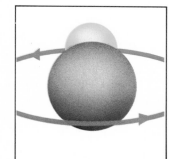

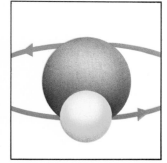

(Left) Variations of Algol. When the fainter star passes in front of the brighter (1 and 3) there is a marked drop in brightness. When the fainter star is hidden (2 and 4) the drop is very slight. With Algol, the eclipses are partial only.

FRIEDRICH BESSEL
THE DISTANCES OF THE STARS

By the start of the 18th century a great deal had been learned about the stars, but one major problem remained: how far were they? The solution was eventually given by the German astronomer Friedrich Bessel.

Bessel was born in 1784. His father worked as a government official, and young Friedrich was sent to work in an exporting company. This did not suit him at all, and before long he decided to throw up his safe but uninspiring post. He became a good linguist, and also showed an aptitude for mathematics. In 1804 he wrote a paper about the movements of Halley's Comet, and by good fortune, sent it to Dr Heinrich Olbers—a physician who was one of the leading German amateur astronomers, and was known for his generosity and kindness. Olbers sent the paper to Johann Schröter, who had a private observatory; Schröter was impressed, and invited Bessel to become his assistant. Then, in 1808, the Prussian Government decided to build a large observatory at Königsberg (the first in Germany), and Bessel was appointed Director. He remained at Königsberg for the rest of his life.

He proved to be a capable administrator as well as an expert observer. In particular he drew up an accurate catalogue of 50,000 stars, and then turned attention to ways of measuring their distances.

The obvious method was that of parallax. If a nearby star were observed at opposite ends of the Earth's orbit—that is to say, at an interval of six months—it would appear slightly displaced relative to the background stars. The first thing to do was to select a suitable star. Bessel chose 61 Cygni, in the Swan, which is just visible with the naked eye; it has a comparatively large proper motion, and is also a wide

binary. After a long series of observations, he found that 61 Cygni showed an annual parallax of 0.3 seconds of arc, corresponding to a distance of 10.3 light-years. As the real distance is 10.8 light-years, Bessel's result was remarkably correct. Other star distances were measured at about the same time, by Henderson in South Africa and F.G.W. Struve in Estonia, but Bessel was the first to announce his results, and so he has the honour of priority.

He also found that the stars Sirius and Procyon show slight irregularities in their proper motions, which he believed to be due to faint companion stars. Again he was correct, though

the companions—both White Dwarfs—were not actually seen until years later. Another investigation of Bessel's concerned the movements of Uranus, and he might well have been the first to locate Neptune but for the death of his assistant, Flemming, followed by his own illness. He died at Königsberg in 1846.

Perhaps the best comment upon Bessel was given by the ever-generous Dr Olbers. He said that in measuring the distance of 61 Cygni, Bessel had "put our notions about the universe on a sound basis"— and added that his own major contribution to science was his recognition of Bessel's outstanding ability.

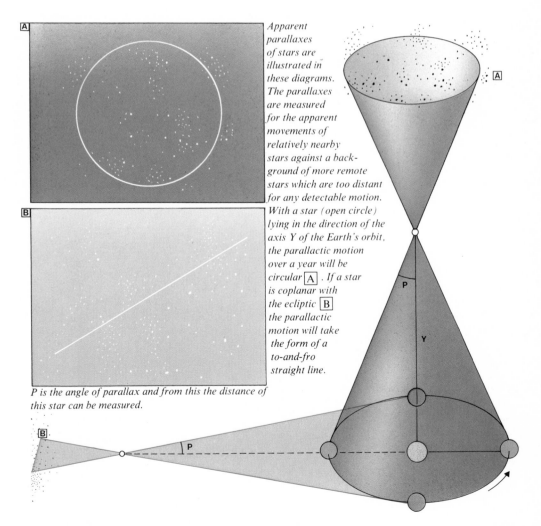

Apparent parallaxes of stars are illustrated in these diagrams. The parallaxes are measured for the apparent movements of relatively nearby stars against a background of more remote stars which are too distant for any detectable motion. With a star (open circle) lying in the direction of the axis Y of the Earth's orbit, the parallactic motion over a year will be circular A *. If a star is coplanar with the ecliptic* B *the parallactic motion will take the form of a to-and-fro straight line.*

P is the angle of parallax and from this the distance of this star can be measured.

JOHANN SCHRÖTER
THE MOON AND THE PLANETS

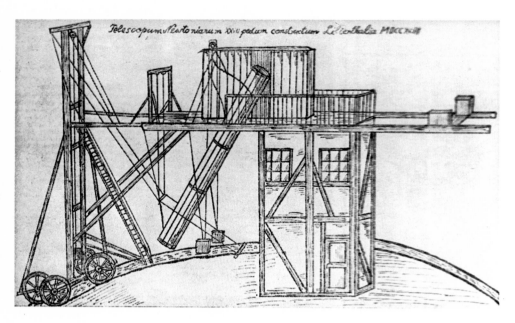

(*Above*) *Schröter's observatory at Lilienthal. His largest telescope was a 19-inch reflector; some of his other telescopes were made by Herschel. The observatory was destroyed when the French sacked Lilienthal.*

There are some astronomers who have never been given the full credit for what they did. One of these is Johann Hieronymus Schröter, who was born at Erfurt, in Germany, in 1745. He accomplished a great deal, and historians in general have been unfair to him.

Schröter was never a professional astronomer, and had no wish to be one. He was trained at Göttingen University for the legal profession, and showed himself to be honest and capable, so that in 1778 he was appointed Chief Magistrate of the little town of Lilienthal, near Bremen. Here he set up his own observatory, and began a long series of observations of the Moon and planets. It has been suggested that his telescopes were of poor quality. This may have been true of the largest instrument, a 19-inch reflector by Schräder of Kiel—about whom we know little except that he was very deaf. But it is certainly not true of the other telescopes, because some of them were made by no less a person than William Herschel. Schröter and Herschel never actually met, but they had

frequent correspondence with each other, which—except on one isolated occasion—was very friendly.

Schröter was particularly interested in the Moon, and he made thousands of lunar drawings. He measured the heights of the mountains very accurately, and also studied the rills, which are crack-like features; a winding valley near the brilliant crater Aristarchus is now known as Schröter's Valley in his honour. He made excellent drawings of Mars and Venus, and was responsible for some important discoveries. For example, he recorded the "Ashen Light", the faint luminosity of the night side of Venus, which is now thought to

be due to electrical effects in the planet's upper atmosphere.

Lilienthal became very much of an astronomical centre. It was here, in 1800, that the "celestial police" met to organize the search for the missing planet between Mars and Jupiter—a search which led to the discovery of the first four asteroids. Schröter was president of the Committee, and another member was the great amateur Dr Heinrich Olbers, who discovered Asteroid No.2 (Pallas) in 1802, and No. 4 (Vesta) in 1807.

The criticisms of Schröter are of two kinds. First, it has been claimed that his drawings were unreliable, This is definitely untrue. He was admittedly a

clumsy artist, but clumsiness is a very different thing from inaccuracy. Secondly, it is said that he misinterpreted much of what he saw. This is correct in the case of Mars, because he believed that the dark markings on the planet's surface were mere clouds; he also thought that the Moon had a fairly dense atmosphere—though he was not nearly so extreme as William Herschel, who was convinced that the Sun was inhabited! But Schröter was quite right in his belief that the surface of Venus is permanently hidden by clouds.

Schröter continued his work until 1813, but then disaster struck. War was raging between France and Prussia; Lilienthal was captured by the French, and Schröter's observatory was destroyed, together with all his notes and unpublished observations. Even the telescopes were plundered, because their tubes were made of brass, and the soldiers believed them to be gold. The loss could never be made good. Schröter did his best, but he was too old to start again, and in 1816 he died. It was a sad end to a noble career.

Schröter was friendly and popular. He showed this very plainly when William Herschel published an attack on him with regard to the existence of high mountains which Schröter had reported on Venus. The attack was certainly not typical of Herschel, but it could easily have led to an open quarrel. Luckily it did not do so, because Schröter's reply was calm, dignified and courteous; before long the two were again corresponding on the usual cordial way. Certainly the Lilienthal astronomer deserves to be remembered as one of the greatest pioneers in the study of the surfaces of the Moon and the planets.

(Above) The Schröter Valley on the Moon, photographed from Apollo 15. This is a great winding valley close to the crater Herodotus, which lies close to the brilliant crater Aristarchus. The Valley is easily visible with a small telescope. Schröter also has a lunar crater named after him, but this is in another part of the Moon.

(Below) Some of Schröter's drawings of Mars; the V-shaped Syrtis Major is clearly seen. Schröter's drawings of the planet were better than any previously made, though admittedly he misinterpreted them, and believed the dark features to be due to clouds.

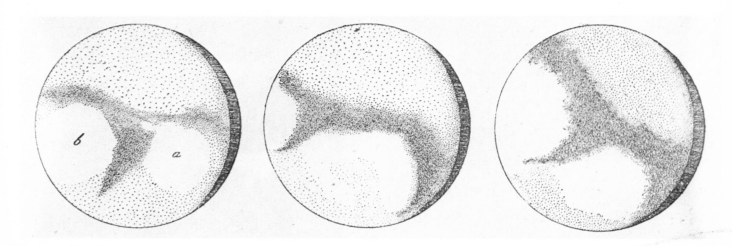

JOSEPH FRAUNHOFER
THE SPECTRUM OF THE SUN

Early astronomers had to depend upon observations made with the naked eye alone. Then came the telescope, and this was in turn followed by the spectroscope, which splits up lights and tells us a great deal about its nature. The first spectra were produced by Isaac Newton in 1666, but the greatest of the spectroscopic pioneers was Joseph von Fraunhofer.

Fraunhofer's career, like Tycho's, reads rather like a boy's novel. He was born at Straubing, in Bavaria, in 1787. Both his parents died when he was very young, and he had little schooling; at the age of fourteen he was apprenticed to a Munich looking-glass maker named Weichselberger, and for a time his life was desperately unhappy. We often hear about cruel masters and ill-treated apprentices, but in Fraunhofer's case this was perfectly true, and to make matters worse his health was always poor. Then came a remarkable stroke of luck. The ramshackle house in which he was lodging collapsed without warning, and he was trapped in the ruins. The rescue operations was watched by the Elector of Bavaria, who just happened to be driving past, and for some reason or other he decided to befriend the boy. He gave Fraunhofer enough money to buy his release from Weichselberger, and to educate himself. Before long he was able to join the workshop of the famous Swiss glass-maker Pierre Guinaud, and showed that he had exceptional skill. His reputation spread; in 1806 he went to the Munich Optical Institute, and became its Director only seventeen years later.

William Herschel had concentrated upon reflectors with metal mirrors. Fraunhofer, naturally enough, preferred refractors, and he made lenses which were much the best of their time. In 1817 he completed a magnificent $9\frac{1}{2}$in object-glass which was bought by the Russian Government for the observatory at Dorpat, in Estonia, and used for a telescope which was employed by F.G.W. Struve to make the first really accurate measurements of double stars. It was, incidentally, the first telescope to be mechanically driven, so that it could track the celestial bodies as they were carried across the sky because of the rotation of the Earth.

But it is for his spectroscopic work that Fraunhofer is best remembered. He passed sunlight through a narrow slit and then through a glass prism, spreading it out into a rainbow band of colours from red to violet; he found that the band was crossed by dark lines, which are still often called the Fraunhofer lines. We now know that each line is the trademark of some particular element or group of elements, so that by studying them we can tell what materials are present in the Sun. Fraunhofer measured the positions of over 300 of the lines, and so provided the basis for all future work.

Sadly, his health failed; he contracted tuberculosis, and in 1826 he died. He was less than forty years old. Had he lived for longer, he would certainly have achieved even greater things.

Joseph Fraunhofer; contemporary portrait.

(Below) Production of a spectrum. The light from the Sun passes through a glass prism and is spread out into a rainbow band, from red at the long-wave end through to violet at the short-wave end. Using a prism and a slit in this way, Fraunhofer studied and mapped the dark absorption lines which are still often known as the Fraunhofer lines.

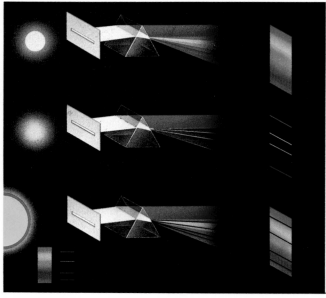

WILLIAM BOND
THE FIRST AMERICAN OBSERVATORY

For many years the United States has been one of the leading nations in astronomical science. It was not always so; until well into the 19th century there were no major observatories there, and few notable astronomers (though David Rittenhouse, who died in 1796, was one). The real American pioneers were the two Bonds, William Cranch and his son George Phillips.

William Cranch Bond was born at Falmouth, in Maine, in 1789. He did not come of a rich family, and his education was, to put it mildly, sketchy; but he went to work in a watchmaker's shop, and soon showed his skill. Then, in 1806, he observed an eclipse of the Sun, and from that time on astronomy was his chief interest. In 1811 he was an independent discoverer of the great comet of that year, one of the most brilliant ever seen. Four years later he paid a visit to England, and the authorities at Harvard College asked him to make a survey of observatories there, with a view to setting up one for themselves.

Bond duly made his report. Meanwhile he made his own observatory; it was modest by present-day standards, but it was better than anything else in the United States at that time, and Bond turned himself into a first-class observer. His son George was born in 1825, and from an early age he and his father worked closely together.

In 1839 the Harvard authorities invited Bond senior to move his observatory lock, stock and barrel to the University. Clearly this was a good move; the Harvard College Observatory was officially opened in 1844, with Bond as Director, and was equipped with a 15in refractor—the first major American telescope.

Important discoveries were soon made. In 1848 the Bonds

(Above) Saturn, drawn by Paul Doherty with a 15-inch reflector. The main divisions in the rings are well shown.
(Left) Harvard College Observatory, the first important observatory in the United States.

found Hyperion, the seventh satellite of Saturn; in 1850 they discovered Saturn's Crêpe Ring, which is semi-transparent, and lies closer to the planet than the two main rings. Traces of it had been seen before, but the Bonds were the first to recognize its nature. By a twist of fate, the English amateur William Lassell independently discovered both Hyperion and the Crêpe Ring—in each case a few nights after the Bonds.

All in all, the important work

carried out during those early days at Harvard was in astronomical photography. In 1851 the Bonds, together with F. Whipple, obtained the first images of a star (Vega); later they photographed the first double star (Mizar), and they also obtained excellent pictures of the Moon. When William Cranch Bond died in 1858, George succeeded him as Director of the Harvard College Observatory, though he too died only seven years later. He was fully his father's equal

as an observer, and is credited with the discovery of eleven comets.

Ever since then the Harvard College Observatory has been in the forefront of research; the work of the Bonds will never be forgotten.

PROBES TO JUPITER

(Inset) Jupiter, from Voyager 1.
Note the cloud belts and the Great
Red Spot. Far more detail is shown
than can be detected from Earth.
(Below) Jupiter as a crescent, from
Voyager. From Earth, for obvious
reasons, the planet can never be seen
as a crescent.

It was natural to begin the direct exploration of the Solar System with the inner
planets, which can be reached in a matter of
months. The giant worlds are so much
further away that a journey there takes
much longer—between one and two years
for Jupiter—and there are all kinds of addi-

tional problems, mainly concerned with
power supply and the transmission of data.
(Solar cells are of little use in the remote
parts of the Solar System, where there is so
great a lack of sunlight.) It is therefore distinctly surprising that all the four outer-
planet probes so far dispatched have been

(Right) The Great Red Spot, from Voyager 2. The structure is well shown; the Spot is a whirling storm—a feature of Jovian "meteorology".

successful, and have indeed achieved more than the planners dared to hope.

The first vehicles were Pioneer 10, launched in March 1972, and its twin Pioneer 11, which followed in April 1973. Pioneer 10 made its rendezvous with Jupiter in December 1973, and Pioneer 11 almost exactly a year later. Pioneer 10 by-passed Jupiter at 81,000 miles, and nearly met with disaster, because the radiation danger proved to be much greater than had been expected, and the instruments were in danger of being put permanently out of action. Hasty modifications were made to the trajectory of Pioneer 11, enabling it to pass quickly over the Jovian equator, where the radiation was at its most intense. Excellent pictures were obtained, together with a wealth of additional information. Pioneer 11 had power to spare; it was swung back across the Solar System to a rendezvous with Saturn in September 1979. Both probes are now on their way out of the Solar System, and both are still in contact. It is hoped that they will be tracked until well into the 1990s, when they will have reached the heliopause—the boundary of the region in which the solar wind is detectable.

Next came Voyagers 1 and 2, launched in 1977. Actually, Voyager 2 departed first, on 20 August, to be followed by its twin on 5 September; but Voyager 1 was travelling in a more economical path, and made its pass of Jupiter on 5 March 1979, while Voyager 2 did not rendezvous until the following 9 July. The results were even more spectacular than with the Pioneers, because the four major satellites were surveyed as well as the planet itself, and we had our first views of the active sulphur volcanoes of Io, the strange cracks on Europa, and the icy craters of Ganymede and Callisto, as well as Jupiter's strange, dark ring which is so unlike the magnificent system of Saturn.

Voyager 2 then went on to an encounter with Uranus in 1986.

There had been fears that the probes would be damaged during the passage through the asteroid belt. If this had happened, nothing could have been done about it; the large asteroids were known, and could be avoided, but many of the smaller ones are beyond our visual range. Fortunately there were no problems on this score, so, that either we have been very lucky or else—more probably—the danger is really much less than had been anticipated.

(Left) The strange world of Io. The surface is red, and sulphur-coated; there are violently active volcanoes. Nothing of the sort had been expected. In view of this activity, and the fact that Io moves in the thick of Jupiter's radiation zones, it is safe to say that any thought of a manned expedition there is out of the question.

(**Above**) Europa, from Voyager 2. There are virtually no craters; there is almost no surface relief, and it has been said that Europa resembles a "cracked eggshell". There have even been suggestions that there may be an ocean below the outer crust, though no doubt Europa has a silicate core.

(**Below**) One of the early views of Europa, from Voyager 1. Voyager 1 did not approach the satellite as closely as its twin.

(*Above*) Valhalla, a large ringed structure on Callisto, seen from Voyager 2. Valhalla and a smaller but similar structure, Asgard, are the main features on Callisto, but there are craters in profusion, and indeed Callisto is the most heavily cratered world known to us. The surface is ancient; nothing has happened there since the very early days of the existence of the Solar System. There could be no greater contrast than that between the icy, changeless Callisto and the violently active world of Io.

(*Above*) Ganymede, largest satellite in the Solar System. There are icy craters and "grooves", together with a large dark region now called Galileo Regio. The surface is totally inert, though there is evidence of some tectonic activity in the remote past.

(*Right*) Jupiter's thin, dark ring, not visible from Earth.

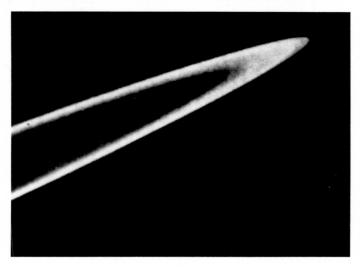

BEER AND MÄDLER
THE MOON-CHARTERS

As the science of photography advanced, a famous French astronomer, François Arago, forecast that by this new technique it would be possible to complete one of astronomy's most difficult tasks—that of mapping the Moon—"in a few minutes". He was wrong; the project was not finished until the 1960s, when the Orbiter space-craft flew round and round the Moon and sent back high-quality pictures of the entire surface. But the foundations had been laid much earlier, first by Schröter and then by two of his countrymen, Wilhelm Beer and Johann von Mädler.

Beer was born in Berlin in 1797. He was trained for a career in banking, and became very successful (as did his brother in another field; he was Meyerbeer, the composer). Wilhelm Beer was interested in astronomy, and for tuition he

(Above) J H von Mädler, the main observer in the partnership of Beer and Mädler. (Below) Two drawings of Mars by Beer and Mädler, 1830-1832; their map of Mars was the best of its time.

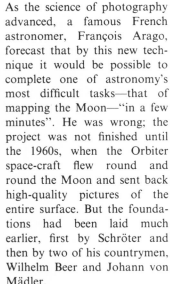

went to Johann von Mädler, who was three years his senior and also came from Berlin. Mädler had lost both his parents when he was eighteen, and did not manage to obtain a place in Berlin University until well in his twenties. He became a teacher, and it was then that he met Beer.

By now Beer had become successful enough to set up a private observatory, equipping it with a fine $3\frac{3}{4}$-inch refractor made for him by Fraunhofer. Beer and Mädler, colleagues rather than pupil and tutor, began serious work in 1830, concentrating upon mapping the surfaces of Mars and the Moon. They recorded considerable detail upon Mars, but it was in lunar studies that they really excelled.

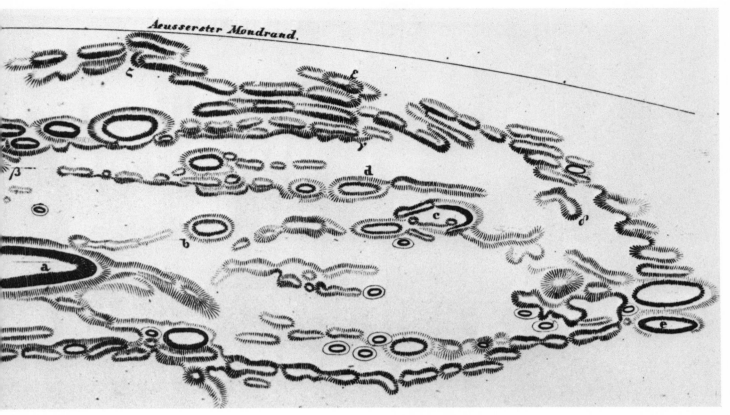

Aeussereter Mondrand.

(**Above**) The lunar crater Bailly, as drawn on 14 November 1835 by Beer and Mädler. Their lunar map remained the best for over 40 years, and was a masterpiece of careful, accurate observation; the telescope used was Beer's 3¾-inch Fraunhofer refractor.

Despite the smallness of the telescope—which was tiny indeed by modern standards—Beer and Mädler produced a chart of the Moon which was a model of careful, painstaking observation. Of course they could not use photography, which was then in a very elementary stage, but for almost ten years they spent every clear, moonlit night at the telescope, mapping, measuring and checking. The result was a map which stands up well in comparison with present-day charts. They also wrote a book, *Der Mond* (The Moon), containing a detailed description of every formation they had seen.

In addition to the mapping work, Beer and Mädler revised the lunar nomenclature, keeping to Riccioli's system but adding

to it and modifying it where necessary. They measured the heights of the Moon's mountains, by the lengths of their shadows, and again the results were very good. Yet ironically, their book and map actually held back further work for some years. It was thought that since the Moon was a changeless world, and Beer and Mädler had mapped it so thoroughly, there was no need to observe it further.

The return to lunar work was again due, though indirectly, to Beer and Mädler. Beer died in 1850; ten years later Mädler left Berlin to go to Dorpat in Estonia, as professor of astronomy and Director of the Observatory, after which he spent most of his time on cosmology (he believed that the

star Alcyone, in the Pleiades star-cluster, was the centre of the Galaxy, though in this he was completely wrong). Mädler retired from Dorpat in 1865, and went back to Germany. A year later Julius Schmidt, Director of the Athens Observatory, announced that a small crater which Beer and Mädler had drawn on the lunar Sea of Serenity, and which they had named Linné, had disappeared, to be replaced by a small pit surrounded by a white patch. Schmidt's claim caused tremendous interest, and once more astronomers turned their telescopes back toward the Moon.

Had it really changed? The answer must be "no". Photographs of it sent back from the space-craft show that it is today a bowl-shaped crater with well-

defined walls; normally, as seen from Earth, it does look like a mere patch, but the crater can sometimes be seen with a small telescope, and in any case we have Mädler's own evidence. After Schmidt's announcement he looked at Linné again, and said that any change "must have come and gone unnoticed" by him, as Linné looked exactly the same in 1868 as he remembered it in 1834. The Moon is indeed a changeless world; nothing much has happened there for the last two thousand million years or so.

Mädler was not a man to remain idle. During his last years he worked hard at writing an authoritative history of astronomy, which he completed shortly before his death in Hanover in March 1874.

THE EARL OF ROSSE
GREAT TELESCOPES AND SPIRAL NEBULAE

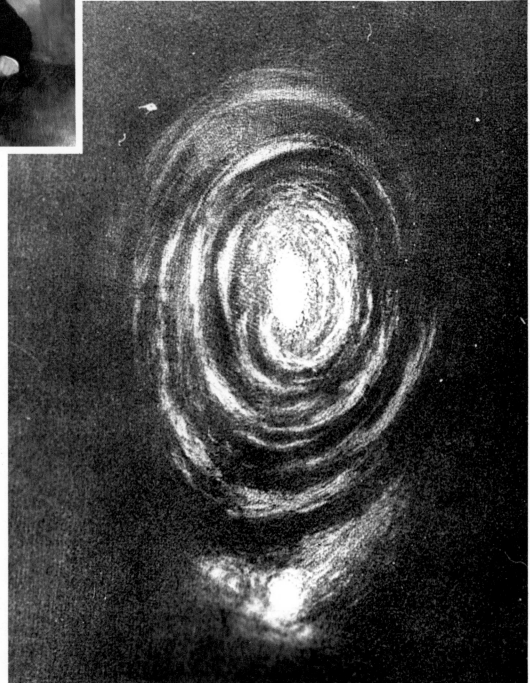

(Left) Portrait of the third Earl of Rosse.
(Below) Lord Rosse's drawing of the Whirlpool Galaxy, M.51, the first spiral to be identified, in 1845. Rosse and his assistants discovered many other spirals; at that time only the Birr reflector was powerful enough to show their forms.

A century ago, where was the world's largest telescope? Surprisingly, not in America or on the European mainland. It was to be found at Birr Castle, in the centre of Ireland, and it was the work of one man—the third Earl of Rosse.

Lord Rosse (known as Lord Oxmantown until he succeeded to the title) was born in 1800, and was educated first at Trinity College, where he obtained a first-class degree in mathematics, and then at Magdalen College, Oxford. We may suppose that at an early stage he realized that science was to be his main interest, but he was also aware of his public duties, and in 1823 he entered Parliament as Member for King's County. As a parliamentarian he was highly effective, but his true political career ended in 1834; two years later his parents handed over Birr Castle and retired to Sussex, mainly because of the better climate there.

By then the story of Birr astronomy had begun, and Lord Oxmantown, as he then was, had published his first papers as early as 1828. But his aim was to build a large teles-scope, and in 1839 he completed a 36in reflector, setting it up in the grounds of the picturesque castle. It was a complete success, but it was only a start. The next task was to make a telescope with a mirror no less than 72in in diameter—much larger than anything previously built.

Lord Rosse had no helpers, apart from workers on his estate whom he trained. He even constructed a forge in which to cast the metal blank for the mirror (in those days it was quite impossible to make glass disks of such a size). Finally all was ready, and according to an eye-witness, Dr Romney Robinson of Armagh, "the sublime beauty can never be forgotten by those who were so fortunate as to be present. Above, the sky, crowded with stars and illuminated by a most brilliant moon, seemed to look down. Below, the furnaces poured out huge columns of yellow flame". It must have been awe-inspiring.

Once the disk had been cast, Lord Rosse shaped it to the correct form for a telescope mirror—a very difficult task, during which he developed new methods which are still standard practice today. But there were equal problems ahead. If Lord Rosse had tried to make the telescope fully steerable, so that it could point to anywhere in the sky, he would have failed. A lesser man would have attempted it. Lord Rosse was too wise. Instead, he mounted the huge tube between two massive stone walls. This meant that the telescope could see only a narrow slit of the sky, due north-south, but as the Earth's rotation carried all celestial objects across this region the method was good enough.

The telescope was ready for testing in 1845, and at once it

*(**Right**) The 72-inch Birr reflector in its heyday; from a painting made at the time. The 36-inch reflector is in the background. The 36-inch no longer exists, but the 72-inch is being restored.*

was found to be every bit as good as had been hoped. Almost at once Lord Rosse looked at some of the objects which Messier had termed "starry nebulae", and found that they were spiral in form like catherine wheels. We now know that the spirals are not members of our Galaxy, but are independent systems, and that our own Galaxy is itself a spiral. The discovery was of immense importance—though for many years no telescope apart from the 72in was powerful enough to show the spiral shapes.

This was only one of Lord Rosse's achievements. He and his self-trained assistants worked unceasingly, and discovery followed discovery. When Lord Rosse's health began to fail, only a year or two before his death in 1868, his son, who became the fourth Earl, carried on the family tradition.

Much of the success of Birr astronomy stemmed from the character of the third Earl himself. He was always ready to share his work with the world; Birr became an astronomical centre, and it is said that

nobody ever went there without being given the full benefit of Lord Rosse's help and advice. The telescope itself remained in operation until 1908, when it was dismantled; but there are now plans to bring it back into operation, and we have every hope that this will be possible within the next few years.

The Birr Castle story is unique, and the 72in was a tribute to the skill of its maker. Lord Rosse made countless friends during his lifetime; it is unlikely that he can ever have made an enemy.

*(**Right**) Picture of the third Earl of Rosse about to begin an observing session with the 72-inch.*

SIR GEORGE AIRY
"YOU ARE THERE, AREN'T YOU?"

It is a sad fact that some people are remembered for their mistakes rather than their triumphs. This has been the fate of Sir George Airy. His failure to seize the chance of searching for a new planet, Neptune, has tended to obscure the great work he achieved over more than half a century.

He was born at Alnwick, in Northumberland, in 1801, and was educated at Colchester Grammar School before going on to Trinity College, Cambridge, in 1819. He graduated in 1823, and showed that he had quite exceptional mathematical ability, as well as a photographic memory (it is said that he once recited over 2,300 lines of Latin verse by heart). In 1826 he became Professor of Mathematics at Cambridge, and two years later he was appointed Director of the Observatory. There he remained until 1835, when he was called to Greenwich.

The Royal Observatory had been going through a bad patch. The Astronomer Royal, Pond, had done very little, and even the Nautical Almanac had suffered. To be honest it was not entirely Pond's fault, because he was in poor health, but eventually he had to be forced to resign, and it was clear that a strong character was needed to replace him.

Airy was the ideal choice. Between 1835 and 1881 he served as Astronomer Royal—a formidable one at that. He modernized the Observatory, equipping it with the best instruments available (many of which he personally designed; the Airy Transit Circle is still the official reference for "longitude zero" dividing the world into two hemispheres). Airy reduced the vast backlog of observations which had built up over the years, and introduced new and highly efficient programmes; he

worked tirelessly, not only upon astronomy but also upon many projects, including timekeeping and navigation. It was largely through Airy's influence that Greenwich Mean Time became the standard for the whole of Britain, and subsequently for the world.

Airy was a strict disciplinarian. He made his observers stay on duty during nights even when rain was falling, and it is claimed he toured the domes saying, "You are there, aren't you?" He carried his passion for order and method rather too far on occasions; it is certainly true that he once spent a whole day in the Greenwich cellars with a pile of empty boxes, carefully labelling each one "Empty". He was self-opinionated, and was slow to change his mind, which is why he failed to appreciate the importance of the hunt for a new planet. On the whole, it is fair to say that he was admired and respected rather than liked. But that his régime as Astronomer Royal was a success there can be no doubt at all. He lived for another eleven years after his retirement in 1881, and it is said that his ghost still prowls around the grounds after nightfall, saying: "You are there, aren't you?"

(Left) The Airy transit circle at the Old Royal Observatory in Greenwich Park, used as the zero for longitude. It is still in perfect order, though it is no longer in official use.

URBAIN LE VERRIER
THE DISCOVERY OF NEPTUNE

"He may not be the most detestable man in France, but he is certainly the most detested." That was the description of Urbain Le Verrier given by one of his colleagues. It may have been harsh, but we have to admit that there could have been a grain of truth in it!

Le Verrier was born at St. Lô, in Normandy, in 1811, and originally meant to become a chemist; but he was equally interested in astronomy, and after graduating from the École Polytechnique in Paris he came under the influence of Françoise Arago, France's leading astronomer. It was due to Arago that he began studying the irregular movements of the planet Uranus, and it was from Le Verrier's results that the new planet Neptune was discovered in 1846. The discovery was actually made from Berlin Observatory by Johann Galle and Heinrich d'Arrest, but the credit was Le Verrier's, and his reputation was made.

Unknown to Le Verrier, the young English mathematician John Couch Adams had reached the same result rather earlier, but when Adams sent his work to Airy, at Greenwich, nothing was done until too late. The French, particularly Arago, were furious at what they regarded as an attempt to steal

the honour from Le Verrier, and there was almost an international incident, though it is to the credit of both Adams and Le Verrier that they refused to become personally involved.

On Arago's death, in 1854, Le Verrier became Director of the Paris Observatory, and continued to undertake valuable researches. There was, however, one investigation which proved to be fruitless. Le Verrier believed that there must be yet

another planet in the Solar System, moving round the Sun at a distance less than that of Mercury. In 1859 he received a message from an amateur astronomer, Dr Lescarbault, claiming that the planet had actually been seen, passing in transit across the Sun's face, and Le Verrier hastened to the little village of Orgères.

It must have been a strange interview. Lescarbault was also a carpenter; his timekeeper was

an old watch with only one hand, and he recorded his notes in planks of wood, planing them off when he had no further use for them! Apparently Le Verrier began by saying: "It is then you, sir, who pretend to have observed an intra-Mercurial planet, and who have committed the grave offence of keeping your observation secret for nine months. I warn you that I have come here with the intention of doing justice to your pretensions, and of demonstrating that you have been either dishonest or deceived." It is all the more surprising that he came away convinced that the planet really had been seen, and it was even given a name: Vulcan. But we now know that there is no Vulcan; whatever the good doctor saw was certainly not a planet.

At Paris, Le Verrier was universally disliked, and finally, in 1870, he was compelled to resign. He was reinstated two years later when his successor, Delaunay, was drowned in a boating accident off the French coast, but he had to put up with what were tactfully called "restrictions". He died in 1877.

(Below) The refractor used by Galle and D'Arrest to identify Neptune.
(Right) Predicted position of Neptune, according to La Verrier (X) and actual position (N).

WILLIAM HUGGINS
THE MESSAGE OF STARLIGHT

Fraunhofer had studied the spectrum of the Sun, and mapped the dark lines crossing it. This was not too difficult—once the method had been found—because with the Sun there is plenty of light to spare. This is not so for the stars, and the spectroscope has to be combined with an adequate telescope. The two great pioneers of the science we now call astrophysics were Angelo Secchi in Italy, and William Huggins in England.

They came from very different backgrounds. Secchi, a Jesuit priest, was an eminent professional astronomer who

up an observatory and devote all his time to astronomy.

At first he was content with looking at the Moon and planets through his 8-inch refractor, but then came an important new development. In 1859 Kirchhoff and Bunsen, in Germany, succeeded in explaining the so-called Fraunhofer lines in the spectrum of the Sun, identifying them with definite elements or groups of elements. Huggins was fascinated. Surely this kind of research could be applied to other objects too? He contacted a friend, Dr Allan Miller, who was a professor of chemistry, and together they

became Director of the main observatory in Rome; he studied the spectra of over 4,000 stars, dividing them up into several well-defined types. Huggins, on the other hand, was an amateur who began his career not as a scientist, but as a draper.

Huggins was born in 1824. He would have liked to have gone to Cambridge; instead he felt that he had no choice but to go into the family drapery business, finally taking it over. Between 1842 and 1854 most of his attention had to be given to his firm, and astronomy was forced to take second place, though during his boyhood he had bought a telescope and learned his way around the sky. It was only when he sold the business, and with his parents moved to Tulse Hill in Outer London, that he was able to set

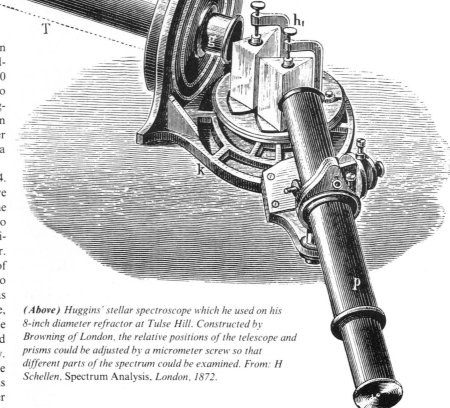

(Above) Huggins' stellar spectroscope which he used on his 8-inch diameter refractor at Tulse Hill. Constructed by Browning of London, the relative positions of the telescope and prisms could be adjusted by a micrometer screw so that different parts of the spectrum could be examined. From: H Schellen, Spectrum Analysis, *London, 1872.*

built a spectroscope which could be fixed on to Huggins' telescope. Almost at once they saw what they had hoped to see. The spectra of the red stars Betelgeux and Aldebaran showed dark lines similar to those of the Sun; so did other stars which were examined shortly afterwards, and in 1863 Huggins and Miller published a pioneering paper, "Lines in the Spectra of some of the Fixed Stars". They were able to find familiar elements such as hydrogen, calcium and iron, though not all the stars showed spectra of the same kind; Huggins guessed that the differences were due mainly to the fact that the stars are not all of the same surface temperature.

Before long Miller's attention was drawn back to chemistry, and for more than ten years Huggins worked alone, but then he made a very happy marriage; his wife shared his interests, and herself became a skilful spectroscopist.

Huggins' method, unlike Secchi's, was to concentrate upon the spectra of the relatively few stars, and examine them in as much detail as possible. In 1868 he made an important discovery. The spectrum of Sirius, the brightest star in the sky, showed lines which were shifted slightly over to the long-wave or red end of the rainbow band; Huggins realized that this was due to the fact that Sirius is moving away from us, so that the lines were red-shifted according to the well-known Doppler effect. Sirius was found to be receding at over 29 miles per second.

Huggins was also the first to study the spectrum of a nebula, and to find that it consisted of isolated bright lines; this showed that the nebula was gaseous, rather than being made up of stars. The planets, on the other hand, showed spectra which were more or less the same as that of the Sun, proving that they shone by reflected sunlight. Neither did Huggins neglect photography, and he was one of the first to obtain photographic stellar spectra.

As the years passed by he became recognised as one of the world's leading authorities. He was elected to the Royal Society in 1865, and he also served as President of the Royal Astronomical Society—a rare honour for an amateur. He was knighted, and was one of the original twelve members of the Order of Merit. From 1870 he was able to observe with two telescopes loaned to him by the Royal Astronomical Society—a 15-inch refractor and an 18-inch reflector—which had far greater light-grasp than his own 8-inch.

Huggins was a charming, modest man, and his family life was always happy. His classic Atlas of Representative Stellar Spectra, completed in 1899, was written jointly with his wife. He remained active until the end of his life in 1910, and took part in a meeting of the Royal Astronomical Society only a week before he died.

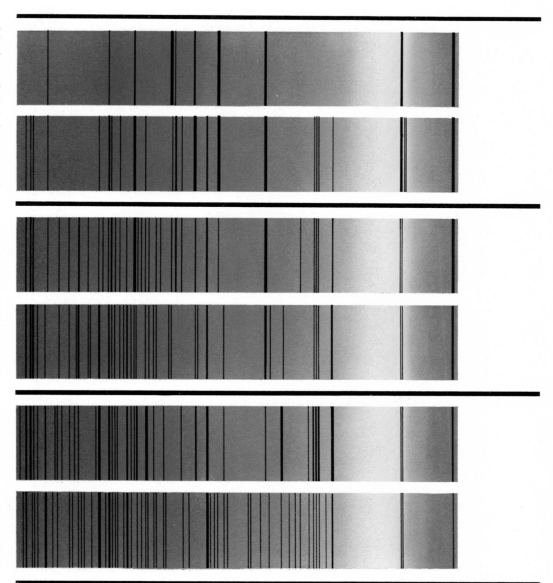

(Above) Stellar spectra. (From top) Hot bluish stars (type B); Sirius white (A); yellowish (F); yellow Capella (G including the Sun); orange Arcturus (K) and orange-red (M, such as Betelgeux in Orion). The dark absorption lines are clearly shown.

GIOVANNI SCHIAPARELLI
COMETS AND CANALS

Everyone who is interested in astronomy knows the name of G V Schiaparelli—but usually for the wrong reason! He is always associated with the non-existent canals of Mars, but his most important work was in connection with comets and meteors.

Schiaparelli was born at Savigliano, in Italy, in 1835, and originally trained as a civil engineer, but after graduating from Turin University he changed over to astronomy, and spent some time working at foreign observatories, first Berlin and then Dorpat. In 1860 he came back to Italy, and was made Director of the Brera Observatory in Milan. The Observatory was not well equipped; most of the telescopes were frankly antiquated, and it was this which made Schiaparelli rather cautious about publishing his results. It was only after 1877 that he was able to use more modern telescopes.

He was particularly interested in comets; he saw Donati's Comet of 1858, which had a

scimitar-like tail and was remarkably beautiful, as well as the Great Comet of 1861, which was brilliant enough to cast shadows. He observed another comet in 1862 (Swift-Tuttle) and began to wonder about the connection with meteors or shooting-stars. Various well-defined showers were known; the August Perseids, the November Leonids and so on.

Schiaparelli found that meteor streams moved in the paths of their "parent" comets, so that they are nothing more nor less than cometary debris. The 1862 comet is the "parent" of the Perseid shower. (The comet itself is thought to have a period of about 120 years, in which case it should have been back in 1982; so far it has not been found, so that either the calcu-

lated period is wrong, or else the comet has come and gone unseen.)

Schiaparelli's first planetary discovery was that of Asteroid No. 69, Hesperia, in 1861. He then turned his attention to Mercury, and attempted to draw a chart of the surface features. This was no easy matter, mainly because Mercury always keeps close to the Sun in the sky; Schiaparelli's method was to observe it in broad daylight, when the planet was high above the horizon.

The fact that his map bore little relation to the truth was not Schiaparelli's fault. He was also wrong in believing that the rotation was "captured"—that is to say, equal to the period of revolution round the Sun (88 Earth-days). If this had been correct, part of Mercury would have been in permanent darkness and another part in permanent sunlight, with only a narrow "twilight zone" in between. It was only in our own time that we have found the real axial rotation period to be no

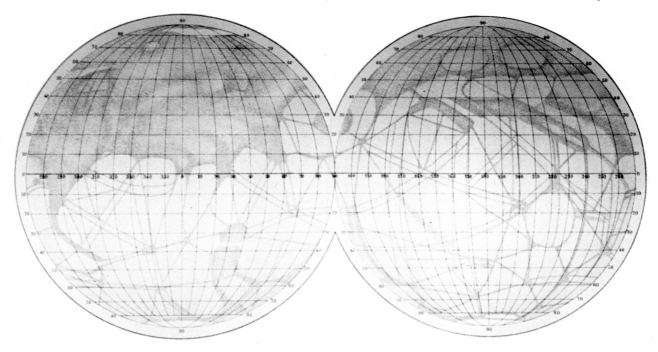

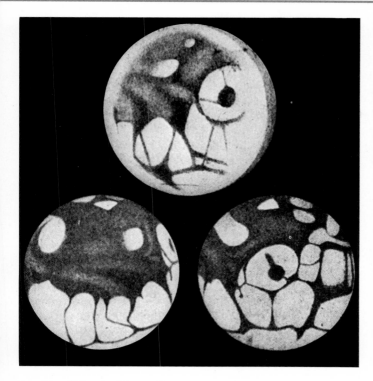

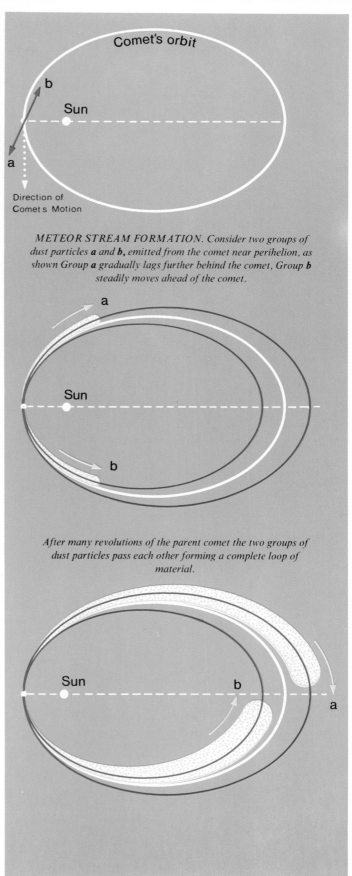

METEOR STREAM FORMATION. *Consider two groups of dust particles* **a** *and* **b**, *emitted from the comet near perihelion, as shown Group* **a** *gradually lags further behind the comet, Group* **b** *steadily moves ahead of the comet.*

After many revolutions of the parent comet the two groups of dust particles pass each other forming a complete loop of material.

Drawings of Mars by Schiaparelli, 1877 to 1879, when he first recorded the complicated canal network. The dark patch near the centre of the lower right-hand drawing is the Solis Lacus or "Lake of the Sun"—then thought to be a true lake.

more than 58½ days.

In 1877 the planet Mars came almost as close to us as it ever can. Better telescopes were installed at Brera, and Schiaparelli began a long series of observations, drawing up a map which was much better than any previously made. He also revised the names of the Martian features, so that, for instance, the V-shaped dark area observed by Huygens in 1659, which had been known as the Kaiser Sea or the Hourglass Sea, became "Syrtis Major"; the old Lockyer Land (named after the pioneer British spectroscopist Norman Lockyer) became "Hellas", or Greece. With minor modifications, the names given by Schiaparelli are still in use today.

But the main feature of the

(Left) Drawings of Mars by Schiaparelli, made between 1882 and 1888, showing the canal network – including double canals.

1877 observations was the detection of long, straight lines crossing the red Martian "deserts". Schiaparelli called them *canali*, or channels, but—inevitably—the term was translated into English as "canals", and canals they remained. He saw them at the next opposition, that of 1879, and also found that some of them had a strange ability to become double. It was not until 1886 that they were reported by anyone else, but after that many astronomers saw them—or thought they did!

What were they? Percival Lowell and others claimed that they were artificial waterways, built by the Martians to pump water from the polar ice-fields to the equator. Schiaparelli was cautious. He did not claim that the canals were artificial, but he did say that he was "very careful not to combat such a suggestion, which contains nothing impossible".

We know now that the canals of Mars do not exist. But the rest of Schiaparelli's work was of immense value, and he deserves to be ranked as one of the leading planetary observers of the nineteenth century.

SIR DAVID GILL
PHOTOGRAPHING THE STARS

The first major observatories in the southern hemisphere were all built in South Africa. And of the nineteenth-century South African-based astronomers, pride of place must surely be given to David Gill, who was Director of the Cape observatory between 1879 and 1906. He was a Scot, born in Aberdeen in 1843, and he never lost his strong Scottish accent. Once, in middle age, he was asked to record a few sentences on a phonograph— the forerunner of the gramophone—and when the recording was played back, it is said that his face was a study. He turned to his wife, and asked: "Do I r-really r-roll my R's like that?" Everyone present burst out laughing.

His father was a watchmaker, and it was natural that Gill should be required to join the family business. He did so, rather reluctantly, training in Switzerland and France before becoming a partner in the firm in 1863. But his main interest was always astronomy; he set up a small observatory, and began to make accurate measurements of double stars. He also experimented with astronomical photography, which was then at an early stage. Eventually he was able to hand over the family business to a competent successor, and to spend the rest of his life in astronomical research. After a spell at a private observatory, during which he went to Mauritius to

Gill's photograph of the bright comet of 1882. It showed many stars as well as the comet – making Gill realize that photography was much the best way to map the sky.

observe a transit of Venus and also made new estimates of the distance of the Sun, he was invited to become Director at the Cape, In 1879 he and his wife arrived in South Africa.

The Cape Observatory was not impressive. The road to it was no more than a muddy cart-track; the grounds were neglected; the retiring astronomer, Stone, had left the building in a state of chaos, and the instruments were ancient and in poor repair. Gill had much to do.

He set to work without delay, and concentrated upon measuring star-distances. Then, in 1882, a bright comet appeared, and Gill decided to photograph it. He fixed a portrait camera to his clock-driven telescope, and exposed the plate for several hours. When he developed it, he was astonished. The comet was well shown—but so were hundreds of stars, and at once Gill realized that this was the best way to map the sky. He ordered a larger lens for his camera, and then organized a world-wide project which resulted in the great Cape Photographic Atlas, showing nearly half a million stars. It was not completed until years after Gill's death, but the credit was his.

Gill was knighted in 1900. He retired from the Cape six years later, and died in London in 1914. He had achieved much; his success was due largely to his energy and his genial, out-going personality. He was totally lacking in self-consciousness, and he made friends wherever he went.

PERCIVAL LOWELL
THE CANALS OF MARS

Percival Lowell was born in Boston in 1855. He came of a wealthy family, and after taking his mathematics degree at Harvard he joined his father's cotton business, which took him to the Far East. He spent ten years there, mainly in Japan, and he also held several official diplomatic posts on behalf of the American Government. On his return home, in 1893, he wrote some excellent books about his travels, and had he wished to do so he could certainly have ended his career as a successful diplomat.

However, he had become fascinated by astronomy—and in particular by the canals of Mars which had been reported by Schiaparelli and others. Lowell was never a man to do things by halves. He carried out extensive tests all over the United States, and decided that Flagstaff, in Arizona, was the best site for a major observatory. He was always well-off financially, and so he was able to establish the observatory which is named after him. It was equipped with a fine 24-inch refractor, and by 1896 Lowell was ready to begin his studies of Mars.

Obviously he was not alone, and the Lowell Observatory had a number of skilled astronomers

and assistants. There was, for example, W H Pickering, noted as a planetary observater, and later there were the Slipher brothers, both of whom made major discoveries. Almost as soon as the telescope was ready, results started to pour out.

Lowell was very definite in his views. He believed the canals to be artificial, and that the Martians—whoever or whatever they were—had built a planet-wide irrigation system to pump

(Right) The Lowell 24-inch refractor, as I photographed it in 1983. It is still in full use at the Lowell Observatory at Flagstaff, Arizona.
(Below) Drawings of Mars made by Lowell in 1894, showing canals.

water from the icy polar caps through to the populated regions nearer the equator. He even wrote that in his view, "That Mars is inhabited by beings of some sort or other is as certain as it is uncertain what those beings may be."

His books and papers caused tremendous interest, but there were many astronomers who disagreed violently with his ideas; moreover, some skilled observers were unable to see the canals at all. It is also fair to say that Lowell was quick-tempered and impatient of criticism. Of course he was wrong about Mars; we now know that there are no canals—they were due to nothing more than tricks of the

eye. Even before Lowell's death, in 1916, support for the super-intelligent "Martians" had declined sharply.

But though Lowell made this one vital mistake, he did much for science. He was a brilliant speaker and writer, a good organizer, and a good mathematician; it was his work which led to the tracking-down of the planet Pluto, from Flagstaff, fourteen years after Lowell died. Today the Observatory is one of the most important in the United States, and it is only right to call it after its founder.

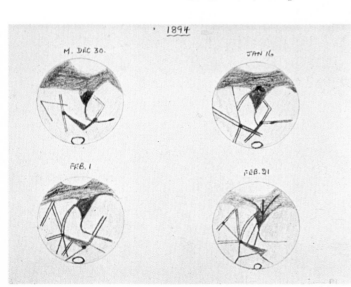

EDWARD BARNARD
THE HOUSE OF COMETS

Edward Emerson Barnard had a background very different from Lowell's. He was born in Nashville, Tennesee, in 1857, and was certainly not rich; when he was only nine years old he had to go to work as a photographer's assistant. Astronomy was always his main interest, and he was anxious to join an observatory; when in his teens he was able to do so, but things were not easy for him, and when he married and wanted his own home there was a desperate shortage of money.

He solved the problem very neatly. A wealthy American had offered a cash prize to anyone who discovered a new comet. Armed with a small telescope, Barnard began searching. he found a comet, and was awarded the prize; then another, and another—each time the bills arrived, a comet came to the rescue, and finally he commented that his house had been built entirely from comets! Altogether he discovered sixteen.

In 1877 he went to the new Lick Observatory, and in 1892, using the 36-inch refractor there, he made an important discovery, that of the tiny fifth satellite of Jupiter—now called Amalthea. He was becoming known for his exceptionally keen sight, and in 1895 he was appointed to the staff of the Yerkes Observatory in Wiscon-

sin, where he was able to use the 40-inch refractor—still the largest telescope of its type in the world.

Not unnaturally, Barnard paid close attention to Mars, but he was quite unable to see the canals reported by Lowell and the Flagstaff observers. Since the canals do not exist, Barnard's failure is understandable, but he did make another observation which was very surprising indeed. He recorded craters on the Martian surface. Yet he refused to publish his results; they seemed so incredible that he was afraid "people would make fun of him", and the page of his notebook is missing.

Much later, in 1917, John

Mellish also recorded craters, but he too was reluctant to publish his observations, and it was not until almost half a century later that the craters were confirmed by the photographs taken by the Mariner 4 space-probe.

Another one of Edward Barnard's important observations concerned the Gegenschein or Counterglow, a faint patch of light in the sky exactly opposite to the Sun. It is now known to be of the same nature as the Zodiacal Light, and to be due to very small, thinly-spread particles in the main plane of the Solar System being lit up by the Sun. Barnard was not the first to see the Gegenschein, but he made very precise observations of it. (It is always very elusive. From England I have seen it only once—in 1942, when the whole country was blacked out as a precaution against German aid-raids.)

Quite apart from his planetary studies, Barnard concentrated upon the Milky Way and upon dark nebulæ. These dark patches are of the same nature as the bright nebulæ, such as that in Orion's Sword, but they are not illuminated by hot stars in or near them, so that they do not shine; they can be

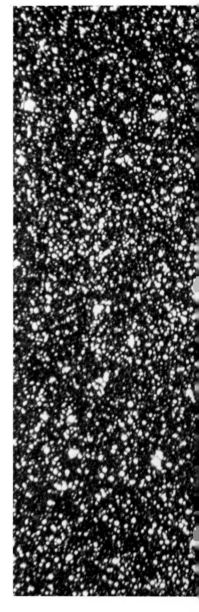

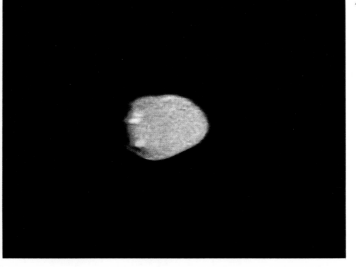

(Above) The dark nebula Barnard 86, showing up as a black patch blotting out the light from objects beyond.
(Left) Amalthea, Jupiter's fifth satellite; Voyager photograph.

traced only because they blot out the light of any objects beyond. The best-known of them is the Coal Sack in the Southern Cross. This is too far south in the sky to be seen from the United States, but Barnard listed many other dark nebulæ, and his catalogue is still used. He knew what they were—unlike Sir William Herschel, who had believed the dark voids to

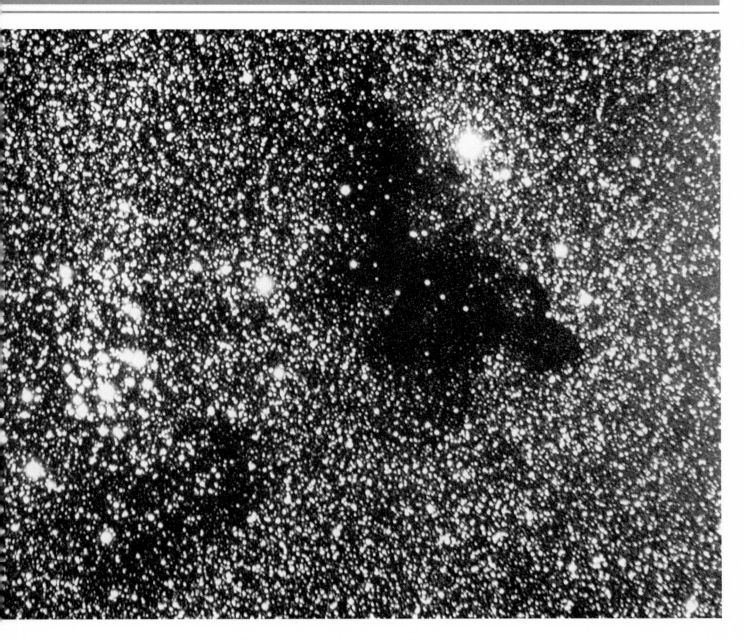

true "holes in the heavens".

In 1916 Barnard measured the individual or proper motion of a faint red star, finding that it takes 180 years to cross the sky by a distance equal to the apparent diameter of the full moon. Barnard's Star, as it is still called, is our nearest stellar neighbour beyond the three members of the Alpha Centauri group, and is a mere six light-years away. Because its movement is not regular, it is believed to be accompanied by at least two planets of about the same size as Jupiter.

As an observer Barnard was outstanding, and he continued his work until shortly before his death in 1923. He was also a man of great charm and modesty, and he had a strong sense of humour, as was shown by his reaction to the famous "comet-seeker hoax". An American newspaper, the *San Francisco Examiner*, published a strange story that Barnard had invented a special telescope capable of discovering comets all by itself, ringing a bell whenever a new comet came into view. The article had clearly been written by an astronomer—and when Barnard sent in a disclaimer, the paper refused to publish it. For years afterwards, Barnard was still having puzzled inquiries about this remarkable instrument. He took it all in good part, and was never able to track down the culprit, though he is on record as saying that he had strong suspicions that the joker responsible was James Keeler, then Director of the Yerkes Observatory.

PROBES TO SATURN AND BEYOND

(Left) *Far view of Saturn from Voyager 1.*

(Above) *Saturn's ring system, seen from Voyager. The shadow of the rings on the disk is very prominent. The rings themselves are highly complicated, with many ringlets and narrow divisions—quite unlike anything which had been suspected. The cause of this structure is not known, but presumably the gravitational pulls of the satellites are involved.*

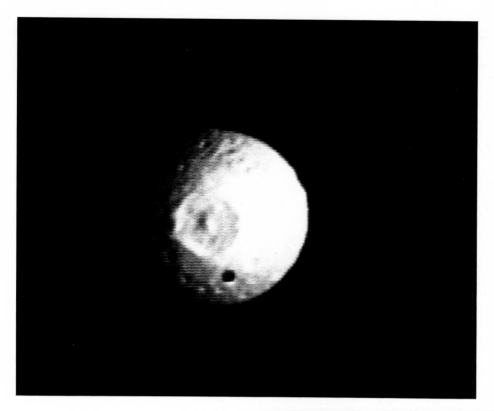

The first Saturn probe was very much an afterthought! Pioneer II had been sent past Jupiter, but was then swung back to an encounter with Saturn on 1 September 1979, providing useful information. There had been a suggestion to send it through the Casini Division in Saturn's rings, but this idea was abandoned, which in the event proved to be a fortunate decision.

The Voyagers were intentional Saturn explorers. Voyager I made its pass on 12 November 1980, at a distance from the planet of some 77,000 miles. Nobody who was in Mission Control at the time (as I was) knew quite what to expect; but as the pictures started to come in on television we became more and more incredulous. Instead of being more or less featureless, the rings proved to be made up of thousands of narrow ringlets and gaps; there were strange "spoke-like" markings which seemed to defy all the laws of celestial dynamics, and one external ring, F, was apparently braided. Moreover the Cassini Division was not empty; it contained narrow ringlets, not all of them perfectly circular.

The satellites were equally fascinating, with the main emphasis on Titan. Would the true surface be visible? The answer was no; Titan's dense in nitrogen-rich atmosphere is always cloudy, and we could see nothing apart from the top of a layer of orange "smog". Of the other satellites Mimas was remarkable, with one vast crater dominating the scene. At the Press confer-

(Above) Mimas; an icy satellite, with one vast crater, now named Herschel, which has well-formed walls and a central peak.
(Below) Enceladus, a different kind of satellite; again with an icy surface, but with small, young-looking craters and wide crater-free areas.

ence, one reporter commented "That must be the engine" and certainly Mimas did look a little like the "Death Star" warship in the famous film, *Star Wars*.

Voyager 2 made its pass on 25 August. This time Titan was not covered in detail, but some of the other satellites were well displayed. After its closest approach there was an alarm when some of the pictures were lost—due, it was subsequently found, to jamming of the scan platform carrying the cameras — but the loss was not so serious as was first feared.

After leaving Saturn, the Voyagers went on their separate ways. Voyager 1 had no more encounters, but Voyager 2 by-passed Uranus on 13–14 March 1986, surveying that curious, tilted world and its family of satellites before starting on toward a final rendezvous with Neptune in 1989.

Both Pioneers and both Voyagers carry plaques, which will—it is hoped—tell any alien civilization happening to find them about their world of origin. Of course, this is very much of a "long shot", but it is not absolutely impossible, even though it cannot happen for many centuries. In any case, the probes will never return. They are our first messengers to interstellar, as opposed to interplanenary, space; and they may well continue travelling between the stars long after humanity has vanished from the face of our Earth.

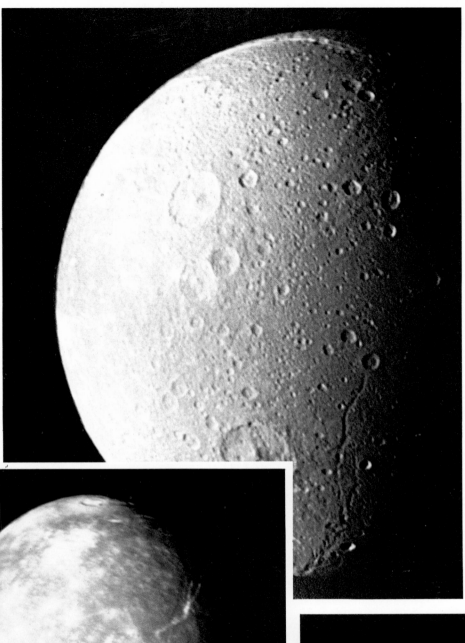

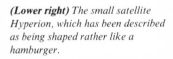

(Left) Dione, slightly larger and much more massive than Tethys. It has an icy surface, with large craters.
(Lower left) Titania, the brightest of Uranus' satellites, photographed from Voyager 2 in January 1986. The surface is icy and cratered, and there is evidence of past crustal activity.

(Lower right) The small satellite Hyperion, which has been described as being shaped rather like a hamburger.

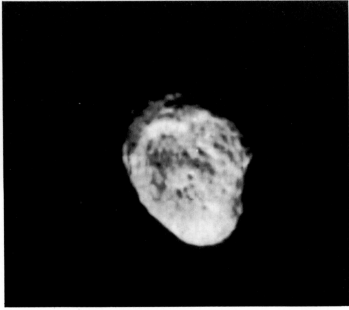

MAX WOLF
PHOTOGRAPHING THE ASTEROIDS

By the end of the last century, photography had taken over from the human eye for most branches of observational astronomy. One of the leaders in these new methods was Maximilian Franz Joseph Wolf (always known as Max Wolf), who was born in Heidelberg in 1863. He went to the university there, and graduated in 1888 with a doctorate in celestial mechanics. He then spent some time in Sweden and the United States before returning to become professor of Astronomy at Heidelberg and Director of the new observatory at Königstuhl, a position which he retained for the rest of his life.

Wolf was an enthusiastic comet-hunter, and made his first discovery in 1883. The comet was periodical, and comes back every $8\frac{1}{2}$ years; it has now been seen at 13 returns, though it is very faint. Later Wolf discovered two more comets, and he was the first to photograph Halley's Comet at the return of 1909-10. But his main contribution was in studying asteroids.

Ceres, the first asteroid, had been found in 1801; three more had followed within the next few years as a result of the activities of the "celestial police", after which there was a lull until 1845, when Hencke detected Asteroid No. 5, Astræa. Subsequently many more of these tiny bodies were found, but hunting for them was very time-consuming, because an asteroid looks exactly like a star, and the only way to identify it is to measure its motion from one night to another. Wolf decided that by photographic techniques he could speed things up, and he worked out an ingenious method.

What he did was to use a camera fixed to a telescope, driving the telescope so that it followed the drift of the stars as they were carried across the sky by virtue of the Earth's rotation. With a time-exposure, therefore, a star would appear as a sharp point of light, but an asteroid would not; it would crawl slowly against its background, and would show up as a streak on the photographic plate. Wolf tried the method out, and it worked. On 20 December 1891 he discovered Asteroid No. 323, now named Brucia. Over the next few decades he found another 231.

Only Karl Reinmuth, with 246 discoveries to his credit, has found more asteroids than Wolf did.

Most of the asteroids keep strictly to the region between the orbits of Mars and Jupiter, but there are some which swing away from the main swarm, and may approach the Earth. The first of these, 433 Eros, was found by Witt, from Berlin, in 1898. Next came 719 Albert, discovered by Palisa from Vienna in 1911; it has a period of 4.4 years, but is only a mile or two in diameter, and it has been lost, so that we have no real idea of where it is now. Then, in 1918, Max Wolf found 887 Alinda, with a period of four years. It is not much larger than Albert, and it was "mislaid" for years, but it was picked up again in 1969, and its orbit is so well known today that there is little fear of our losing it again.

Even more interesting was Wolf's discovery, in 1906, of an asteroid far outside the main zone. No. 588, Achilles, moves in the same orbit as Jupiter, but

(**Right**) *Halley's Comet at the 1910 return; Wolf was the first to see it. This is the comet's head, as photographed from Mount Wilson.*

keeps well away from the giant planet, and is in no danger of being swallowed up. Achilles was the first of the so-called Trojan asteroids, which form two groups—one 60 degrees ahead of Jupiter, the other 60 degrees behind. Achilles is over 100 miles in diameter, but its great distance from us makes it extremely faint.

Like Barnard, Wolf was also very interested in dark nebulæ, and discovered many of them. He also found some bright nebulæ, including the "North American" Nebula in Cygnus, near Deneb, whose shape really does bear a slight resemblance to that of the North American continent. It is not a difficult object, and binoculars will show it, but its surface brightness is low, which is why it had been overlooked before Wolf drew attention to it.

Max Wolf was active until shortly before his death, at Heidelberg, in 1932. Quite apart from his contributions to astronomical photography, he developed a new kind of instrument for measuring exposed plates, and he was a tireless and inspiring teacher, universally popular with his students—of whom there were many. A lunar crater has been named in his honour, and Asteroid No. 827 is called "Wolfiana".

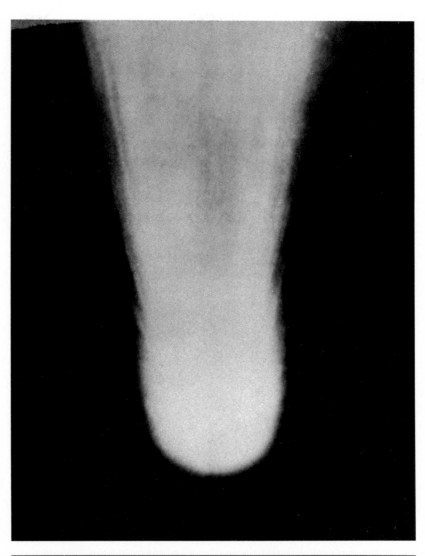

(**Right**) *Asteroid trails; photograph by Max Wolf. The camera was following the Earth's rotation, so the stars appear as points; but the asteroids move during the time-exposure, and show up as short streaks.*

GEORGE ELLERY HALE
THE GREAT REFLECTORS

The 200-inch Hale reflector at Palomar, showing an observer in the prime focus cage and the reflecting surface of the main mirror.

Some astronomers are remembered for their observational skills; others for their theoretical work; others for developing new instruments and new techniques. George Ellery Hale qualifies on all three counts. He was a brilliant observer, who was the first to recognize the importance of the magnetic fields of sun-spots; he was equally eminent as a theorist, and he invented the spectroheliograph, used for studying the Sun in the light of one element only. Perhaps most important of all, he was personally responsible for the setting-up of the world's largest telescopes.

He was born in 1868, in Chicago, and soon showed that he had exceptional ability. His father provided him with a well-equipped private observatory, and it was here that he made his first serious observations, mainly in connection with the Sun. However, he was anxious to use larger telescopes, and he began planning a major observatory. He made contact with Charles Tyson Yerkes, a Chicago industrialist, and persuaded him to put up the money for a 40-inch refractor, larger than any other telescope of that type ever made. The Yerkes Observatory, at Williams Bay in Wisconsin, was completed in 1879, with Hale as its first Director.

The 40-inch was an instant success, and it is still used on every clear night, but Hale was not satisfied. His constant call was for "More light!" and he realized that the real future of astronomy lay not with the refractor, but with the reflector. Lenses have to be supported round their edges, and if they are too heavy they will distort under their own weight, making them useless. On the other hand, the mirror for a reflector can be supported on its back. Moreover, a large mirror is much easier to make than a large lens.

Hale had a positive genius for persuading friendly millionaires to finance his schemes—something which was much easier eighty years ago than it is today! He contacted John D Hooker,

of Los Angeles, with a proposal for another new observatory, to be equipped with a really large reflector. Hooker agreed, and the result was a 60-inch telescope, much the most powerful ever built. The site chosen was Mount Wilson, overlooking Los Angeles, where some special telescopes for studying the Sun had already been installed. Next came the Mount Wilson 100-inch "Hooker" reflector, which was completed in 1917, and which for 30 years was in a class of its own; with it, in the 1920s, Edwin Hubble was to make the classic observations which showed that the so-called "starry nebulæ" really were independent galaxies, far beyond our Milky Way system.

Still Hale was not satisfied. The 100-inch had proved its value; why not build a 200-inch? Money was always a problem and at first the outlook was gloomy; but Hale was patient—and persuasive. Finally the blank for the 200-inch mirror was cast. Unfortunately there were long delays, and Hale did not live to see the telescope completed; he died in 1938, and

*(**Right**) The 60-foot tower telescope at Mount Wilson, used for studying the Sun.*

it was not for another ten years that the 200-inch reflector on top of Palomar Mountain was finally brought into operation.

The importance of these two great reflectors cannot be over-estimated. Just as the 100-inch had been supreme in its day, so too was the 200-inch, and it enabled men to see further into space than had ever been possible before. Even now there is only one larger telescope, the Russian 236-inch, which, to be honest, has never been a real success.

There is one note of sadness. The city of Los Angeles has grown, and the brilliant lights have made "seeing" conditions on Mount Wilson deteriorate so much that in 1985 the telescopes there were closed down. There is a real danger that the Mount Wilson Observatory will be permanently given up, which will be a tragedy for science. Palomar, further away from large cities, is in no immediate danger of suffering the same fate, though the whole situation is being carefully watched.

Hale's patience, enthusiasm and pleasant personality made him an ideal organizer. He faced immense difficulties, and overcame them all. One famous story — certainly true — shows that he was never a man to neglect an opportunity. He was anxious to contact the appropriate millionaire; both he and his "victim" were guests at the same dinner party, but at different tables, which did not suit Hale at all; so he calmly switched the labels, placing himself next to the millionaire. Before the dinner-party was over, the idea of a new giant telescope was already being discussed.

EUGENIOS ANTONIADI
MAPPING THE PLANETS

With E M Antoniadi, one of the greatest of all planetary observers before the age of space-probes, we come to the first astronomer in this book whom I knew personally. He was Greek, but was actually born in Constantinople, in 1870, and became a French citizen in 1928. He had close British connections, and was for many years Director of the Mars Section of the British Astronomical Association.

Antoniadi spent most of his life in France. In 1893 he arrived at the Juvisy Observatory, which was privately owned and run by Camille Flammarion, a well known popularizer of astronomy and also the founder of the Société Astronomique de France; it was here that he began his main work—mapping the planets. Flammarion and Antoniadi were not in the least alike. Flammarion was something of a mystic, and his ideas tended to be decidedly unorthodox, while Antoniadi was extremely practical—and also very outspoken. However, the two worked well together, and continued to do so even after Antoniadi left Juvisy and went to the Meudon Observatory, outside Paris, where he was able to use the 33-inch refractor there (one of the world's largest) to great effect.

Mars was a particular interest. Antoniadi was no believer in Lowell's canals, which he compared sarcastically with a spider's web, though he did believe that the streaks drawn by Schiaparelli had "a basis of reality". He drew a new map of Mars which was much better than any previously made, and he modified the names of the Martian features, though there have been some further modifications since, for example, what he called the *Lacus* Phœnicis, or the Lake of the Phœnix, is now known to be

(Below) Dome of the 33-inch refractor at the Observatory of Meudon, outside Paris. This is one of the largest and best telescopes of its type in the world.

a huge volcano, so that it has been renamed Phœnicis *Mons*. Antoniadi wrote a classic book, *La Planète Mars*, which for some strange reason was never translated into English until I did so in the 1970s—by which time it was of historical value only.

Antoniadi also studied Mercury and Venus. Like most other observers he believed that they had "captured" rotations, so that each planet would keep the same face turned perma-

nently towards the Sun. In this he was wrong, though he can hardly be blamed. Venus shows no permanent surface markings, while those of Mercury are very difficult to glimpse even with a telescope as powerful as the Meudon refractor. He also believed that Mercury had an atmosphere dense enough to support clouds, which also is incorrect. In 1934 he wrote a book, *La Planète Mercure*, which again remained unavailable in English until I translated

it 30 years later.

In addition to his observational work, Antoniadi was also a noted historian of science, and translated many of the ancient texts into French; he wrote a standard book on Egyptian astronomy. He remained at Meudon after the outbreak of war, and died there in 1944.

HERTZSPRUNG AND RUSSELL
THE H-R DIAGRAMS

How are stars born, how do they develop, and how do they die? By now we believe that we have found many of the answers to these questions, though some of the details remain to be cleared up. In this research, great use is made up of what are termed H-R Diagrams, named after two astronomers: Ejnar Hertzsprung of Denmark and Henry Norris Russell of the United States.

Ejnar Hertzsprung was born in Frederiksberg in 1873. Originally he meant to study chemistry, and did indeed graduate as a chemical engineer, but he then decided to devote his life to astronomy. He worked first in Copenhagen, and then in Göttingen and Potsdam before going to Leiden, in Holland, to become Director of the Observatory there.

Hertzsprung made a careful examination of different kinds of stars, and found something very interesting. Red stars were either very brilliant or else very dim; red stars of about the same power as our Sun did not seem

to exist — there were either red giants, or red dwarfs. There were similar, though less marked, giant and dwarf divisions for orange and yellow stars, but not for stars which were very hot and either white or bluish-white. In 1906 Hertzsprung drew up a diagram in which he plotted the stars according to their luminosities and their colours. Most of the stars lay on a band stretching from the top left of the diagram down to the bottom right—the so-called Main Sequence—while very powerful red stars, such as Betelgeux in Orion, lay

(Below) Hertzsprung-Russell of HR Diagram. The vertical scale indicates luminosity in terms of the Sun; the horizontal scale indicates surface temperature. The Main Sequence extends from upper left to lower right; the giant branch is to the upper right, and while dwarfs, such as Sirus B, to the lower left.

on the "giant branch" to the upper right.

Hertzsprung published his results, but not in a major scientific journal, and for some years they were not widely known. Then, in 1913, a similar diagram was produced by Henry Norris Russell, who had been born at Oyster Bay, New York, in 1877 and had become Director of the Princeton Observatory. Russell's work was independent, and so we now call the Diagrams after the names of both men.

Could they indicate an evolutionary sequence? So Russell believed. On his theory, a star would begin by condensing out of a nebula as a large, cool red giant; as it shrank, under the influence of gravity, it would heat up and join the Main Sequence to the upper left, after which it would cool and shrink as it slipped down the Main Sequence, ending up as a red dwarf. It all looked very plausible, but in fact things are not so straightforward. A star is indeed born inside a nebula, but it joins the Main Sequence at a point depending upon its original mass, remaining there for most of its "life". Only when it has used up its main sources of nuclear energy does it move into the red giant branch. This means that, for instance, Betelgeux is ancient rather than young.

Russell made many other contributions to astronomy before his death in 1957. So too did Hertzsprung—among them a method of estimating stellar distances by examination of the spectra of the stars. He lived until 1967, and when I last met him, when he was well over 90, he was as active and alert as ever. He was a great teacher, and a charming, modest man. Neither he nor Russell will ever be forgotten; their Diagrams are of vital importance in present-day astronomy.

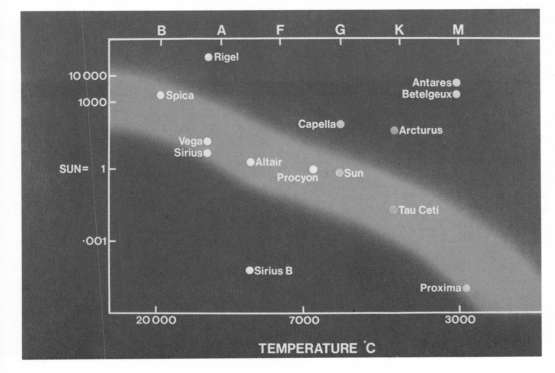

KARL SCHWARZSCHILD
BLACK HOLES IN SPACE

There can be few people today who have not heard something about Black Holes—which, if they really exist (as most astronomers believe) must be the most extraordinary objects in the entire universe. Rather surprisingly, they were first discussed almost 70 years ago by the German astronomer Karl Schwarzschild, who became one of the many victims of the first world war.

Schwarzschild was born in Frankfurt in 1873. His family was Jewish, and his father had become a wealthy businessman. His childhood was peaceful and happy; he graduated from Strasbourg University, and then went to Munich, after which he worked successively at observatories in Vienna and Göttingen. In 1902, when he was still in his twenties, he became Director of the Göttingen Observatory, and finally, in 1909, went on to take charge of the observatory at Potsdam.

By then he was already well known (his first theoretical paper had been published when he was only sixteen). He was a splendid lecturer as well as an observer and a theorist; he had the happy knack of making "difficult" scientific problems sound easy, so that he was in great demand. When the war came, he volunteered for active service, and was sent to the Eastern Front to calculate trajectories for long-range shells. While in Russia he caught a skin disease from which he died. It was a sad end to a brilliant career.

Among all Schwarzschild's important papers, perhaps the most fascinating was written only shortly before he died. In it, he put forward the first ideas about what we now term Black Holes.

The gravitational pull of a body depends upon its mass.

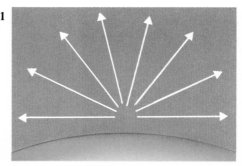

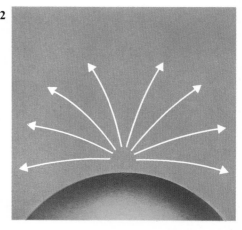

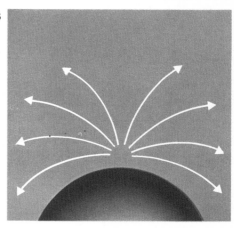

(Right) Formation of a black hole. As the massive star collapses when its "fuel" is exhausted. It becomes denser and denser and its escape velocity becomes stronger and stronger. At first (1) the star has not yet started to collapse, and all the light-rays and other emissions can leave its surface in the usual way. At (2) the collapse has begun, and although the light-rays can still escape they are perceptibly bent. By (3) the collapse is well under way, and the distortion of the paths of the light-rays is very evident. By (4) the distortion has become so great that the light-rays are bent back on themselves and cannot leave the star at all; a black hole has been formed. We know nothing about the final fate of the old collapsed star or "collapsar". There have even been suggestions that it may crush itself out of existence.

(Far right) A pulsar is a rotating neutron star, whose axis of rotation does not coincide with the magnetic axis. Near the star the plasma rotates, sending out radio waves in beams. Beyond this the plasma is stationary. It is now agreed that it is the magnetic field of the rotating neutron star that generates the pulses as it turns over and over. The mechanism is related to the region some distance from the neutron star where the magnetic field would have to travel at the speed of light to keep up with the rotation.

The escape velocity—that is to say, the speed needed to break free from the body—depends also upon size. The escape velocity of the Earth is 7 miles per second; that of the smaller, less massive Moon is only 1½ miles per second (which is why the Moon has been unable to hold on to any atmosphere it may once have had). What will happen with a body which is extremely small and extremely massive? The escape velocity will become as great as the speed of light: 186,000, miles per second. In this case nothing can break free, because light is the fastest thing in the universe.

Schwarzschild began to consider this possibility. Of course, it is not so straightforward as it may sound, because what we are really considering is the "distortion of space", but the end result would be clear-cut; the central body would surround itself with a kind of forbidden region, cut off from the rest of the universe. In other words, it would form a Black Hole.

This could happen with a very massive star which uses up all its reserves of energy. When it collapses, under the influence of gravity, the collapse is so violent that nothing can stop it. When the critical or "Schwarzschild" radius is reached, a Black Hole is produced. For a star, the radius may be a few miles; for the Sun it would be less than two miles, and for the Earth less than an inch—though in fact neither the Sun nor the Earth could ever form a Black Hole, because they are not massive enough.

Obviously we cannot see Black Holes, and we can detect them only by their pulls upon bodies which we can observe. The best case is that of Cygnus X-1, in the constellation of the Swan, which is made up of a visible giant star associated with an invisible companion which has 15 times the Sun's mass (as we can 'tell from the way in which the system is moving). If the companion is a Black Hole, it must be pulling material away from the visible star; before the material is sucked into the Black Hole it is so strongly heated that it emits a stream of X-rays. This is why the system is called Cygnus X-1.

What happens inside a Black Hole is a mystery. All the ordinary laws of science, and of common-sense, break down. Many theories have been put forward, some of them decidedly far-fetched, but as yet we cannot pretend to know.

The Black Hole concept was only one of Karl Schwarzschild's important contributions to science, and in 1960 the Berlin Academy of Sciences officially named him as the greatest German astronomer of modern times. He was awarded a posthumous Iron Cross for his wartime work; it was tragic that his career was cut short.

VESTO MELVIN SLIPHER
PLANETS AND SPIRAL NEBULAE

When Percival Lowell died suddenly in 1917, he was succeeded as Director at Flagstaff by his senior assistant, Vesto Melvin Slipher. Slipher's younger brother, Earl Carl, was also a member of the Lowell Observatory staff, and produced some magnificent pictures of the planets which were the best of their time.

V M Slipher was born in Indiana in 1875. He graduated from Indiana University, and in 1902 Lowell invited him to come to Flagstaff, where he remained for the rest of his life. He was always popular, and he made an extremely efficient and hard-working Director.

His first important work was in measuring the rotation periods of the planets, including Uranus—no easy task, because Uranus shows virtually no markings upon its pale, greenish disk. Slipher gave a value of 10.7 hours. This was much too small, but at least he showed that Uranus, like Jupiter and Saturn, spins round much more rapidly than the Earth. He also carried out spectroscopic observations of the planets; in 1929 he organized a new search for a planet beyond Neptune, and it was at his invitation that Clyde Tombaugh, then a young amateur, joined the Observatory staff. Only a year later Pluto was found not far from the position which Lowell had worked out for it, though we must admit that luck may have played a great part in that discovery.

However, Slipher's main work was in connection with the spiral nebulæ, which he began in 1912, using the Lowell 24-inch refractor. At that time it was generally believed that the spirals were members of the Milky Way system rather than being independent galaxies, and Slipher set out to measure the speeds at which they were moving. His method was to use the well-known Doppler effect. If the lines in the spectrum of a luminous body are shifted over to the long-wave or red end of the rainbow band, it means that the body is receding; with a few exceptions, Slipher found that for the spirals the shifts were indeed to the red. This was an indication that they lay beyond the edge of the Milky Way, though it was not for another ten years that Edwin Hubble, using the Mount Wilson reflector, was able to give final proof. The gaseous nebulæ, of course, were quite different, and Slipher found that some of them, including the lovely nebula in the Pleiades cluster, shine by reflected starlight.

V M Slipher died in 1969, five years after his brother. He had played a great part in raising Flagstaff to the status of a major observatory, and for this alone he deserves great credit.

(*Left*) The 13-in refractor used by Clyde Tombaugh in the search for Pluto.

(*Right*) Pluto at its discovery in 1930. The over-exposed star is Delta Geminorum. Pluto is indicated by the arrows. Photograph by Clyde Tombaugh.

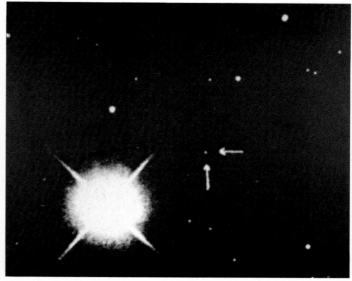

BERNHARD SCHMIDT
THE NEW CAMERAS

Bernhard Schmidt is one of the more curious characters in the history of astronomy. He was what we nowadays often call a "loner"; he disliked working with a team, and he was always moody and unpredictable. Near the end of his life he lost his reason. But he made one absolutely fundamental discovery which has revolutionized our whole methods of observation.

He was an Estonian, born on the island of Naissaar in 1879. (At that time Estonia, as now, was controlled by the Russians.) Schmidt's family was poor, and the boy had little formal schooling, but he was always interested in science, and he was an enthusiastic experimenter. His

(*Left*) *The United Kingdom Schmidt (UKS) at Siding Spring in New South Wales, Australia. This is one of the world's largest Schmidt telescopes, and has recently been used for the photographic survey of the entire sky accessible from Australia.*

first telescope lens was made by taking an ordinary bottle, cutting out its bottom, and using sand to grind it into the correct optical shape. Another of his early ventures was less successful. He made some gunpowder, packed it into a metal tube and then set light to it, presumably to see what would happen. The result was that he blew off part of his right arm, after which he decided that explosives were best left alone.

When he was 21 he went to the Institute of Technology at Gothenburg, in Sweden, to study engineering; he next moved on to Mittweida in Germany, and after graduating he stayed there, making mirrors and lenses for telescopes. He was exceptionally skilful, and in 1905 produced a first-class 15-inch mirror for the Potsdam

Observatory. He continued his work, mainly on his own, until 1926, when Schorr, Director of the Hamburg Observatory, invited him to join the staff. Schmidt accepted, but he still preferred working alone, and he was never an easy man to know.

His major contribution came during his period at Hamburg. The main trouble about photographing the sky with an ordinary telescope is that the field of view is small, and it takes many exposures to cover even a limited area. Schmidt found the remedy. He used a spherical mirror, and combined it with a special glass plate, fixed in the upper part of the telescope tube, to correct the errors caused by the spherical shape of the mirror. These "Schmidt telescopes" (or Schmidt cameras) made it possible to photograph wide areas of the sky with a single plate, with the definition remaining sharp right up to the edge of the field. The first instruments of this sort were purely photographic, but later they were developed for visual use as well. Today, no observatory is complete without its Schmidt telescope.

Schmidt died in 1935, in an asylum for the insane in Hamburg. His life was not happy, but the optical system which he developed was one of the most important of modern times.

LEONID KULIK
THE GREAT SIBERIAN EXPLOSION

At dawn on 30 June, 1908, there was a tremendous explosion in the remote region of Tunguska, in Siberia. Some solid body plunged into the atmosphere from outer space; it shot through the sky, becoming brighter than the Sun, and then hit the ground, blowing pine-trees flat over a wide area. The bang was heard hundreds of miles away, and there was an intense blast of heat, while the shock was felt by earthquake-recorders in many parts of the world. Had the object struck a city, the death-roll would have been colossal. It was sheer luck that the Tunguska region is uninhabited, so that the only casualties were the herds of reindeer.

What was it? The first man to make a serious effort to find out was Leonid Kulik, who had been born in 1883 at Tartu in Estonia, and had studied science at Kazan University. In 1904 he joined the Russian Army during the war against Japan, but later he ran into trouble with the authorities; he was arrested and tried for "revolutionary activities", and served a term of imprisonment. After 1912 he went to the Ural Mountains as a forester, and met a leading Russian astronomer, E L Krinov, who described him as "a vibrant, cultured man around whom young people flocked"; he was always ready to speak his mind, but his honesty and skill were res-

pected. It was due to Krinov that he was able to obtain a position in the Mineralogical Museum at the city then known as Petrograd, now as Leningrad. While there he became interested in meteorites, and his attention was drawn to the remarkable event of 1908.

Nobody had been to the scene of the explosion; things in Russia had been much too unsettled. Kulik decided to find out. After a great deal of planning, he and a small party went to the site in 1927, travelling mainly by horse-drawn sled; on the way they met an old farmer, S B Semenov, who told them that at the moment of the explosion "there was so much heat that my shirt was almost burned off my back", even though he had been many miles away.

When Kulik and his companions finally arrived, they saw evidence of devastation, with giant pine-trees still lying flat in the manner of match-sticks. Yet there was no crater, and no sign of any iron or stony material which would indicate the fall of a meteorite. It was all very puzzling.

Between 1927 and 1938 Kulik led several more expeditions to Tunguska. Then, in 1941, the Germans invaded the Soviet Union. Kulik went to war once more; he was wounded, captured, and imprisoned in one of Hitler's camps where he died on 24 April 1942.

Kulik remained certain that the object which hit Siberia really was a meteorite. Today it seems more likely that it was icy in nature, either part of a comet or else the head of a small comet which had approached unseen. For the moment, the Tunguska explosion remains in a class of its own, and what knowledge we have of it is due mainly to Leonid Kulik.

(Left) Debris left by the Siberian impact of 1908, and first studied in detail by Kulik from 1927. The objects which look like matchsticks are in fact tall pine-trees, blown flat by the explosion.

SIR ARTHUR EDDINGTON
THE MAKE-UP OF A STAR

*(**Left**) Sir Arthur Eddington. (**Right**) Albert Einstein. Eddington was one of the main supporters of relativity theory—and, it was said, one of the very few people who genuinely understood it in the early days of relativistic research.*

If there were a vote for the greatest British astronomer of the twentieth century, the choice of many people would be Arthur Stanley Eddington, who was born at Kendal in Cumbria in 1882 and was educated first at Owen's College, Manchester, and then at Trinity College, Cambridge, where he graduated in 1905. Shortly afterwards he was appointed Chief Assistant at the Royal Greenwich Observatory, and it was there that he began his outstanding work in theoretical astrophysics. His final move was to Cambridge, in 1913, where he became Professor of Astronomy and Director of the University Observatory.

Eddington was particularly interested in the constitution of the stars. He realized that in a star's globe there are two main forces at work: gravitation (tending to make the star shrink) and radiation pressure (tending to make it expand). In a normal star these two forces balance each other out. Eddington also showed that the life-story of a star depends upon its original mass; the more massive the star, the greater its luminosity, and the quicker it evolves. Cosmic searchlights such as Rigel in Orion run through their careers much more quickly than milder stars such as the Sun.

Between 1905 and 1916 Albert Einstein published his classic papers on the theory of relativity. In Eddington he found an enthusiastic supporter—and also one of the very few people who really understood the theory; Einstein commented that it was worth learning the English language purely for the pleasure of talking to him.

As well as being a theorist, Eddington was also a practical observer. He led two eclipse expeditions, of which the second was of particular importance. According to relativity, the apparent position of a star in the sky will be slightly changed if it lies almost in the same direction as the Sun; the rays coming from it will be "bent" as they pass close to the Sun's limb. Under normal conditions stars cannot be seen in the daytime, but during the fleeting moments of a total solar eclipse the sky becomes dark, and the stars shine out. This was why Eddington went to the island of Principe, off the coast of West Africa, on 29 May 1919. The measurements were made, and they gave perfect confirmation of Einstein's theory.

During his lifetime Eddington received many honours, including a knighthood. Quite apart from his theoretical work, he was a brilliant speaker and popular writer; he was the first great astronomer to broadcast regularly, and he made his last broadcast not long before he died in November 1944. He was a Quaker, and unfailingly friendly and courteous. I know this, as I first met him when I was aged 15—and he paid me the compliment of talking to me as though I had been his equal.

Eddington's dedication to science was total, and was neatly summed up by the Astronomer Royal, Dyson, just before the 1919 eclipse expedition. One of the assistants asked what would happen if the measurements failed to confirm Einstein's ideas. Dyson thought for a few moments, and then said, solemnly: "In that case Professor Eddington will go mad, and you will have to return alone." It is therefore just as well that the experiment was a success!

HARLOW SHAPLEY
THE SIZE OF THE GALAXY

Map of the Milky Way (Lund Observatory). Shapley was the first to measure its diameter accurately. The two Clouds of Magellan are shown to the lower right.

PHOTOGRAPHIC MAGNITUDES

In 1962, during one of my television broadcasts in the BBC *Sky at Night* series (which began in 1957, and has continued monthly ever since) I discussed the size of the Galaxy in which we live. My own contribution was not, however, very great, because with me in the studio was the man who had actually solved the problem 40 years earlier: Harlow Shapley.

Shapley was born in Missouri in 1885. His father was a farmer; his early education was somewhat sketchy, and at the age of 16 he left school and became a newspaper reporter in Kansas. He intended to make this his career, but when he tried to enrol at the University of Missouri's School of Journalism he found that he would have to wait for a full year before being accepted. Not wanting to waste time, he decided upon astronomy instead. Therefore, he became an astronomer almost by accident.

After graduating he went to Princeton, and worked with Henry Norris Russell upon studies of double and variable stars. He did valuable work, particularly in showing that the short-period Cepheid variables are pulsating stars rather than eclipsing binaries of the Algol type. He completed his doctorate, and then, in 1914, went to the Mount Wilson Observatory, where he remained for seven years. His next move was to Harvard, as Director of the Observatory. His administration was a great success, and lasted until he retired in 1952, by which time he had turned Harvard into one of the leading astronomical centres of the United States.

During his time at Mount Wilson, Shapley began an investigation into the size and shape of the Galaxy. He concentrated first upon globular clusters, which are huge, regular systems of stars lying round the edge of the Galaxy; the brightest (Omega Centauri and 47 Tucanæ) lie in the far south of the sky, but one globular, Messier 13 in Hercules, is an object visible by the naked eye from northern latitudes. Most of the globulars contain short-period variable stars, and Shapley was able to measure their distances, because it had already been found that these stars "give away" their luminosities by the way in which they behave—and as soon as the luminosities are known, the distances can be worked out. Shapley realized that the variables, and hence the clusters, were very remote indeed, and he was able to give a good estimate of the diameter of the Galaxy, now known to be of the order of 100,000 light-years. Another discovery was that the globulars are not spread uniformly around the sky; they are commonest in the south, particularly in the region of Sagittarius, the Archer. Shapley correctly claimed that this was because we lie well away from the centre of the Galaxy and therefore have a "lop-sided" view of the globular clusters. We are in fact around 30,000 light-years from the galactic nucleus, which lies beyond the Sagittarius star-clouds.

There was another major problem. Were the spiral systems and other "starry nebulæ" members of our Galaxy, or were they external? Shapley believed that they were compar-atively minor features of our Galaxy, but other astronomers, notably Heber D. Curtis, did not agree. In 1920 there was a famous debate between Shapley on the one side, and Curtis on the other. Curtis believed the starry nebulæ to be true galax-ies, and that our own Galaxy was much smaller than Shapley had claimed. The result of the debate must go down as an honourable draw. Shapley was right about the size of our Galaxy, but Curtis was correct in saying that the spirals lie far beyond. A few years later Hubble, using the Mount Wil-son 100-inch reflector, gave the final proof that it was Shapley who had been wrong.

Shapley had no hesitation in accepting the verdict, and went on to make new discoveries. For example, he identified two dwarf galaxies (one in Sculptor, the other in Fornax) which are members of our Local Group. This is a collection of galaxies, including our own, the Andro-meda and Triangulum spirals, and more than two dozen smaller systems, which are not receding from each other.

On his retirement, Shapley turned his attention to the inter-national organization of astronomy as well as writing various books, some of which were mainly philosophical. He was one of the best of all "popular" writers. It was there-fore all the more surprising that in 1950 he was accused of Com-munist sympathies, and was "investigated" during the witch-hunt headed by the infamous Senator Joseph McCarthy. Needless to say, he was soon cleared.

Shapley remained active almost to the end of his life. He was a charming companion; I am proud to have known him.

LUND OBSERVATORY
MARTIN KESKÜLA
TATJANA KESKÜLA

EXPLORING THE GALAXY

Human beings tend to be conceited. We like to believe that we are exceptional, living in an exceptional place. Yet astronomical research has shown that nothing could be further from the truth, and at last we may be starting to learn our lesson.

Originally it was thought that the Earth must be the centre of all things. There were of course some doubters, notably Aristarchus of Samos, but the conceited view was generally held up to the time of the great revolution in outlook which began with Copernicus and ended with Newton. But what about the Sun? Surely it merited some special rank?

Bessel's measurement of the first star-distance, in 1838, disposed of this idea. There was nothing remarkable about the Sun, and within a few decades it had become very clear that some of the familiar stars of our skies outshine the Sun as effectively as a lighthouse will outshine a glow-worm. But then came the problem of the Milky Way. Could it be the only system in

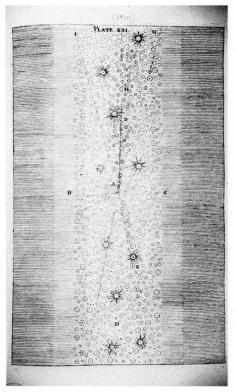

(Left) General shape of the Milky Way system, according to Wright; from his Original Theory.

(Left) Rich star-field in the Milky Way. The stars are not genuinely crowded together; the Milky Way band is a line of sight effect!

(Above) The Pleiades star-cluster. The principal stars are hot and white, and much younger than the Sun; there is also a lovely reflection nebula in the cluster. Most of the stars in this photograph are, of course, either in the foreground or the background, though the Pleiades cluster contains several hundreds of members.

(Right) Diagram of the Galaxy. The overall diameter is about 100,000 light-years. The Galaxy is rotating; the Sun has a period of 225,000,000 years—often called the "cosmic year".

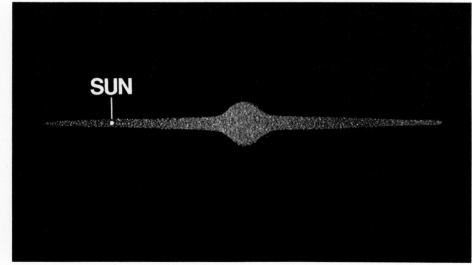

the universe?

Herschel had shown that the Milky Way band is a line of sight effect, and in our own time Harlow Shapley measured its size by studies of the globular clusters. (He also showed that the Sun is nowhere near the centre of the Galaxy; we are around 30,000 light-years from the galactic nucleus.) Then came Hubble's work with the 100-inch Hooker reflector, elevating the spirals to the rank of external galaxies. Yet there was one disquieting fact. Our Galaxy appeared to be much larger than any other. Could we be in a privileged position after all?

It was not until after the war that the answer was found. Baade discovered the major error in the Cepheid variable scale, proving that the galaxies were twice as remote as had been believed. At once everything fell neatly into place; there was nothing unusual about the Milky Way system. It was not even the largest galaxy in our Local Group; that distinction belongs to the Andromeda Spiral.

The Local Group itself contains more than thirty galaxies, a few of which are large while the rest are dwarfs. Yet it is very small as "clusters of galaxies" go. The Virgo cluster of galaxies contains many thousands of members, some of the true giants—such as the huge elliptical system Messier 87. Our Local Group may well be a minor unit of the Virgo Cluster, and there are now suggestions that the Virgo Cluster itself may be nothing more than a part of an even grander "supercluster".

Quite apart from this, our Galaxy is normal in shape. During the war, when the Low Countries were overrun by the Germans, all astronomical work in Holland came to a stop—except for the theorists. One of these was H. van de Hulst, who found that clouds of cold hydrogen spread through the Galaxy should radiate at a wavelength of 21 centimetres. After the end of the war, two American radio astronomers, Ewen and Purcell, identified the 21-cm radiation, and were able to map the hydrogen clouds. They showed that our Galaxy is a perfectly conventional spiral.

There are still some who believe that at least Mankind is unique. This may be so, but the odds are very much against it. We have no longer any reason for conceit.

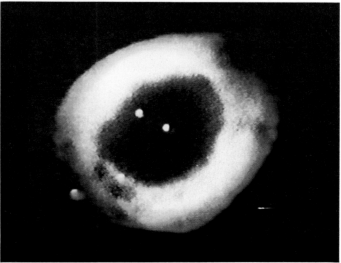

(**Above**) Messier 13, the great globular cluster in Hercules. It is easily visible with binoculars, and can just be seen with the naked eye. It is over 22,000 light-years away, and contains at least half a million stars.

(**Left**) Messier 57, the Ring Nebula in Lyra. It was the first planetary nebula to be discovered, by A Darquier in 1779. The distance is probably considerably less than 2,000 light-years. The faint central star is a strange bluish object, extremely dense and with a surface temperature of about 100,000°C. This photograph was taken with the Palomar 200-inch reflector.

(**Above**) M.42, the Great Nebula in Orion—a stellar nursery, in which fresh stars are being born. It shines because of the hot stars in and near it; deep inside it are some powerful infra-red sources which may be very luminous stars, completely hidden from us.

(**Left**) A photograph of the Orion molecular cloud, taken from IRAS, the Infra-Red Astronomical Satellite, in 1983. The visible Orion Nebula is part of this molecular cloud.

HUBBLE AND HUMASON
THE EXPANDING UNIVERSE

The greatest revolution in astronomy since the time of Galileo was due largely to Edwin Powell Hubble. He was born in Missouri in 1889, and went to the University of Chicago, where he met George Ellery Hale, but his first intention was to study law, and after graduating he actually practised for a few months before deciding that astronomy was to be his life's work. In 1914 he went to the Yerkes Observatory as an assistant. When America entered the war, in 1917, Hubble volunteered—he had excellent physique, and was a noted amateur boxer—after which he accepted Hale's offer of a position on the Mount Wilson staff. It was here that he spent the rest of his career, interrupted briefly during the Second World War when he served as an expert on ballistics.

Hubble's greatest contribution was his proof that the so-called "starry nebulæ", including the spirals, are independent galaxies. He was able to show this because he was observing with the Mount Wilson 100-inch Hooker reflector, at that time far the most powerful in the world, and he looked for, and found, short-period variable stars in the Andromeda Spiral and other systems (as we know, these variables "give away" their distances by the way in which they change in light) and Hubble realized in 1923 that they were much too remote to belong to our Galaxy. He gave the distance of the Andromeda Spiral as 900,000 light-years, later reduced to 750,000 light-years. This turned out to be an under-estimate, but the vital step had been taken, and the credit was Hubble's.

He went on to measure the distances of many other galaxies, and he divided the systems into definite classes according to their shapes, from loose spirals

(Above) The Mount Wilson 100-inch reflector, used by Hubble to prove that the "starry nebulae" are external galaxies.
(Right) Part of the Andromeda Spiral M.31, showing the resolution into stars; photograph taken with the 100-inch reflector.
(Inserts) Hubble and (far right) Humason.

to galaxies so symmetrical that they looked very like globular clusters. He also found that there was a definite link between the distance of a galaxy and the speed with which it is moving away. The entire universe is expanding. In all this research he was joined by a most remarkable astronomer, Milton la Salle Humason.

Humason's background was

porter. Hale talked to him, and was impressed enough to make him a Night Assistant (not without criticism from other members of the staff, partly because of Humason's complete lack of qualifications but also because the Observatory engineer was his father-in-law). From that time onward Humason's progress was steady. He worked closely with Hubble, and showed himself to be a true expert in handling the delicate equipment; he became a first-class theorist, and in 1961 he even found enough time to discover a comet.

Hubble was essentially practical; Humason has been described as "gentle and friendly". I met them only briefly, but that was certainly my own impression.

Hubble died in 1953, active almost to the end of his life, and recognized as America's greatest astronomer of modern times. The great 84-inch Space Telescope, due to be launched in the near future, has been named in his honour. Humason lived on until 1972. His life-story is not unique—Jean Louis Pons, discoverer of no less than 36 comets, began his career as a doorkeeper at the Marseilles Observatory, in 1799, and ended it as an observatory director—but Milton Humason's achievements are remarkable by any standards.

very different from Hubble's. His formal education was practically nil, but after a camping holiday on Mount Wilson he became very interested in astronomy, and managed to obtain employment at the new Observatory—as a mule driver! He ferried much of the building material up the mountain, along a track which was then very rough, and in 1911 he married the daugher of the Observatory's engineer. During 1917, the year when the 100-inch reflector was brought into operation, he applied for, and obtained, the job of observatory

WALTER BAADE
STELLAR POPULATIONS AND DISTANCES OF GALAXIES

(Below) The Andromeda Spiral, M.31, photographed with the 200-inch Palomar reflector. Baade's work showed it to be twice as remote as had been previously thought.
(Right) Dome of the Palomar reflector; photograph which I took in 1983.

Walter Baade was another European astronomer who carried out his best work in the United States. He was the son of a German schoolmaster, and was born at Schröttinghausen in 1893. He studied at Münster and then at Göttingen University, where he graduated in

1919; he then worked at the Bergedorf Observatory in Hamburg before emigrating to America in 1931. He joined the staff of the Mount Wilson Observatory, and settled down to serious research.

Though interested mainly in the stars, Baade also, paid attention to the Solar System, and discovered two asteroids of exceptional interest. One, Hidalgo, has a curious orbit which carries it from the inner Solar System out almost as far as Saturn. The other, Icarus— discovered in 1948—ventures closer in to the Sun than Mercury, so that at perihelion it must be red-hot. Even today there is only one other known asteroid, Phæthon, which moves closer in than Icarus.

During the Second World War America was blacked-out, and the nights at Mount Wilson were exceptionally dark, so that Baade was able to use the 100-inch reflector and take full advantage of the conditions. (His German origin was no real obstacle, though it is true that for some time the authorities kept a close watch on him.) Baade set out to study individual stars in the centre of the

Andromeda Galaxy, which was something that Hubble had been unable to do. To his surprise, he found that the brightest stars in the nucleus of the spiral were not bluish-white, as had been expected, but old red giants. From this, Baade concluded that there were two definite types of what he called "stellar populations". Population 1 is made up chiefly of young, hot stars, while in Population 2 areas the most luminous stars are red and ancient; spiral arms are mainly Population 1, while the centres of galaxies (and also all the globular clusters) are Population 2. Moreover, Population 1 areas are rich in interstellar gas and dust, so that star formation is still going on, while in Population 2 regions all the available star-producing material has been used up.

The war ended, and Baade transferred from Mount Wilson to Palomar, where the 200-inch Hale reflector was brought into operation. This gave him the opportunity to study very faint variable stars which were beyond the range even of the Mount Wilson telescope. He took every possible precaution,

but even so, as he commented, he "only just got under the fence". Finally he discovered that the short-period variables used by Hubble and Humason to measure the distances of the galaxies were of Population 1 rather than Population 2. This was of tremendous importance, because the Population 1 stars were twice as luminous as those of Population 2—which meant that they were also twice as far away, so that the universe was much larger than had been thought. For instance, the Andromeda Spiral is 2,200,000 light-years away instead of only 750,000. There had been an error of more than one hundred per cent.

Baade announced his findings at a meeting of the Royal Astronomical Society, in London, in 1952. In a brief twenty-minute paper, he calmly doubled the size of the universe. I was there, and I well remember the stunned silence when Baade finished speaking and sat down.

It also followed that our Galaxy is not exceptionally large. It has been regarded as superior to the Andromeda Spiral, but in fact it is smaller; the Andromeda Spiral contains more than our own quota of about 100,000 million stars.

Baade continued his work, not only upon cosmology but also upon the nature and constitution of individual stars. He stayed at Palomar until 1958, but then decided to return to his native country, and become a professor at the University of Göttingen, where he had studied so many years before. He died in 1960. He was a pleasant, friendly person—and he will always be remembered as being the man who demonstrated that our whole picture of the size of the universe had been wildly wrong.

GEORGE GAMOW
THE HOT BIG BANG

In our story of astronomy we have come across quite a number of eccentric characters. Yet another is George Gamow, whose unusual behaviour made many of his colleagues take his ideas less seriously than they ought to have done.

He was Russian, born in Odessa in 1904. At the age of 13 he was given a telescope, and made up his mind there and then to become a scientist. He studied successively at Leningrad, Göttingen, and Copenhagen, and then spent a year in England before being called back to Russia to join the Academy of Sciences at Leningrad. He was not impressed with the Soviet way of life, and when he was allowed to attend a conference in Belgium in 1933 he refused to return home; in fact he never did so. Instead he

went to America, and became Professor of Physics at the University of Colorado, remaining there until he died in 1968.

His first notable success was in 1938, when he showed that the stars shine by nuclear reactions—mainly the conversion of hydrogen into helium. He then turned his attention to the problem of the birth of the universe. It had been suggested that the universe began in a "big bang" thousands of millions of years ago, and has been expanding ever since. Unfortunately there were some awkward facts which could not be easily explained, and Gamow finally decided that the original creation must have been in the form of a "hot big bang". He worked out a full sequence of events, which we now know to have been over-simplified but which

has paved the way for almost all future research in cosmology.

Gamow also believed that we might be able to detect remnants of the hot big bang in the form of weak radiation coming in towards the Earth from all directions. He was correct, though it was not until after his death that the "background radiation" was actually detected. Today we regard it as one of the most powerful arguments in favour of the whole big bang theory.

As well as being a brilliant nuclear physicist, Gamow was also the author of some excellent (and amusing) popular books. It is to my everlasting regret that I never met him.

One example will show why some of his colleagues were cautious about accepting his ideas. He attended an important con-

ference about star-clusters, but slept through all the meetings—not quietly; his snores almost drowned the voices of the speakers. A few days later, the organizer of the conference received a telegram from Gamow which showed that by a brilliant flash of insight he had found a way to measure the ages of the clusters, which is what the conference had been all about. One of the speakers made the acid comment that George Gamow asleep could think much more clearly than any other astronomer who was wide awake!

The cluster of galaxies in Coma; Palomar 200-inch reflector.

KARL JANSKY
THE BIRTH OF RADIO ASTRONOMY

In 1931 a young radio engineer named Karl Jansky was carrying out some unusual experiments on a farm at Holmden, in New Jersey. He was employed by the Bell Telephone Company, and had been instructed to investigate the causes of "static", the irritating hissing and crackling in long-range communications. For this purpose he had built a curious aerial, which moved around on wheels taken from an old Ford car; he had named his aerial the "Merry-go-round". It was while at Holmden that he made a discovery which he certainly did not expect, but which turned out to have far-reaching consequences.

Jansky was of Czech descent, but his father had emigrated to America to become a professor at the University of Wisconsin, so that Karl was an American citizen; he was born in Oklahoma, in 1905. He had taken his physics degree at Wisconsin before joining the Bell Company, and he was known to be a careful and patient experimenter. Static, of course, is the radio operator's worst enemy, and the authorities were anxious to find out as much about it as they could.

Jansky recorded plenty of static, due largely to thunderstorms, but there was another source of noise which puzzled him. It was a weak, steady hiss in the receiver—obviously not close at hand, and not in the least like a thunderstorm. Moreover it seemed to come from a definite region of the sky, and this region moved steadily from day to day. Eventually Jansky found the answer. The hiss came from the Milky Way—more precisely, from the Milky Way in the region of the star-clouds in Sagittarius, beyond which lies the true centre of the Galaxy.

What Jansky had done, in fact, was to pick up radio waves

(Below) Modern radio telescope, the 210-foot "dish" at Parkes, in Australia.

(Left) Jansky's original aerial, the "Merry-go-round," with which he first detected radio waves from the Milky Way.

from space. Whether he realized its full importance is doubtful. He published his results in the following year, and they were fairly widely reported, but nobody showed much interest in following them up apart from an amateur named Grote Reber, who went so far as to build a "dish" aerial to pick up radio emissions from the Sun. In view of what has happened since, it is indeed remarkable that the beginning of radio astronomy caused so little excitement.

It is also very surprising that Jansky himself made little real effort to take matters further. He published a few more papers, but after a year or two he more or less abandoned radio astronomy and turned his attention to other matters. He died of heart disease in New Jersey in 1950.

By then, of course, radio astronomy had started to come to the fore. Various discrete sources had been found—among them the Crab Nebula, in the Bull—and large radio telescopes were being planned. But Jansky had taken no part, and to all intents and purposes his studies of radio waves from the sky ended before the outbreak of war. He deserves great credit for his pioneering work, but one has the feeling that he could have done so much more.

99

GERARD KUIPER
THE PLANETS IN THE SPACE AGE

For a small country, Holland has produced a remarkably large number of famous astronomers. One of them was Gerard Peter Kuiper, who was born at Harenkarspel in 1905. It is true that he spent most of his life in America, emigrating there in 1933 and taking United States citizenship, but he never forgot the country of his birth.

On arrival he went to the Yerkes Observatory, acting as Director from 1947 to 1949 and again from 1957 to 1960. He then left to become Director of the new Lunar and Planetary Laboratory at Tucson in Arizona, of which he was the real founder; it was Kuiper who laid down its policies and was responsible for the research programmes there. It has been said that he could be "difficult", and this may well be true, though I came to know him reasonably well and was always on excellent terms with him.

Unlike so many modern astronomers, Kuiper was interested mainly in the Moon and planets, and at an early stage in his career he drew up a theory of the origin of the Solar System which was very different from the older ideas—according to which the planets had been pulled off the Sun by the action of a passing star. Kuiper's theory had more in common with the "nebular hypothesis" of Laplace, since he believed that the planets were built up gradually from a cloud of dust and gas associated with the young Sun.

He was a skilled spectroscopist, and in 1944 discovered that Titan, Saturn's largest satellite, has an atmosphere. This has been fully confirmed by the Voyager space-craft, though admittedly it is much denser than Kuiper had believed, and is made up chiefly of nitrogen, which of course makes up 78 per cent of the atmosphere of the

Earth. In 1948 he discovered Miranda, the fifth satellite of Uranus, and in 1949 he also found Nereid, the second satellite of Neptune.

It is not often that anyone actually looks through the eyepiece of a giant telescope, but on several occasions Kuiper used the Palomar 200-inch reflector visually. He examined the rings of Saturn, and concluded that the famous Cassini Division was the only genuine gap in them, with the other reported divisions—even Encke's—being mere "ripples". In this he was wrong, and the ring-system has proved to be immensely complex, with thousands of ringlets and narrow spaces. Another visual observation concerned Pluto, whose diameter was uncertain. Kuiper did his best to measure it, and believed it to be almost as great as that of the Earth, though here too he was wrong; Pluto is smaller than the Moon.

When space research began in earnest, with the launching of Russia's first artificial satellite in October 1957, Kuiper played a leading role. At the Lunar and Planetary Laboratory a detailed

photographic atlas of the Moon was produced, and was of immense value in selecting the landing sites for the unmanned lunar probes and, later, the Apollo missions, though it is true that by the mid-1960s all Earth-based mapping of the Moon had been superseded by the results from the unmanned Orbiters. Mars was another of Kuiper's main interests; he had already predicted that the Mar-

(Below) Domes on the summit of Mauna Kea, in Hawaii, at about 14,000 feet. It was Kuiper who originally suggested Mauna Kea as the site for a major observatory.
(Right) The United Kingdom Infra-red Telescope at Mauna Kea.

tian atmosphere would turn out to be composed mainly of carbon dioxide, and the Mariner probes showed him to be correct.

During the planning of the various space-craft Kuiper was always very much to the fore, but his work did not end there. He was also well aware of the importance of Earth-based observations, and he realized that it was essential to select the best possible sites for new telescopes. One of these, he felt, was the Hawaiian volcano of Mauna Kea, and he went there to carry out a preliminary survey.

Mauna Kea is 14,000 feet high; unlike its neighbour Mauna Loa it is extinct (at least, we hope so!). Kuiper was confident that a major observatory could be built there, above the densest part of the Earth's air. He met with considerable opposition, because working in a very tenuous atmosphere causes real problems, but eventually he had his way. By now there are great telescopes on the summit of the volcano, and more are being planned.

Gerard Kuiper died in 1973, so that he lived to see the first lunar landings even though he missed the excitement of the spacecraft to the outer planets. His outstanding contributions have been recognized in many ways; the famous "Kuiper Airborne Observatory" (a telescope carried on a specially-converted aircraft) has been named after him, and so has the first crater to be recognized on the surface of Mercury. The Lunar and Planetary Laboratory continues to flourish, and it owes everything to his guidance in its early days.

YURI GAGARIN
MAN IN SPACE

There are some names which will never be forgotten so long as humanity lasts. One is that of Yuri Alexeyvich Gagarin, who has the distinction of being the first man in space—a record which can never be taken away from him.

Yuri Gagarin was born on 9 March 1934 in the village of Gzhatsk, near Smolensk. There was nothing particularly notable about his family. His father was a carpenter, and was far from rich, so that life was not easy. Altogether there were four children; two were older than Yuri, and one younger.

Just as he was starting school, the Germans invaded Russia. The Smolensk area became a battlefield, and then it was occupied by the Nazis. The older Gagarin children were deported, and somehow or other they managed to survive; Yuri stayed on in Gzhatsk, together with his parents and his younger brother Boris. Food was desperately short, and even grass had to be eaten when nothing else could be found.

When the Germans were finally driven out, Gzhatsk had to be completely rebuilt. A new school arose from the ruins, and Yuri went there; his first task was to learn how to read—rather later than most boys, though it was hardly his fault! He developed a keen interest in science, and while still in his teens he had made enough progress to attend a training course at an apprentices' school near Moscow. He intended to become a metalworker, and did actually qualify as one, but by now his main interest was in flying, and he was able to join a flying club, where he had his first experience of piloting. It took him only a short time to learn, and he was sent to the Orenburg Air Force School, where he graduated as a test pilot. Then, in 1959, he volun-

Gagarin in Vostok 1. *His pioneer flight marked the beginning of the manned exploration of space.*

teered for training as a cosmonaut.

It was an exciting time. Sputnik 1 had already been launched, and at that period the Russians were in the lead so far as space research was concerned. It was fairly obvious that the first manned trip could not be far away (I remember saying so in a television broadcast a few days before it actually happened), and the honour of making it fell to Yuri Gagarin. He was a good choice. He was a skilful pilot; he had a good knowledge of physics and engineering, and he had passed all his training tests with ease, difficult though some of them were. He was physically very fit, and he was also popular and good-looking, which was another point in his favour so far as the Soviet authorities were concerned. Rather naturally, they wanted their first cosmonaut to make a good impression.

At last, on 12 April 1961, all was ready. Gagarin was strapped down in the cramped cabin of his space-ship, Vostok 1, waiting to be hurled beyond the atmosphere. Later, I asked him whether he had felt badly frightened. He replied that he had no time to think about anything except the matter in hand; there was so much to do that he had to concentrate grimly.

Gagarin was launched at 06.07 GMT. When blast-off came, he felt crushing pressure as the space-craft accelerated; during the worst period—fortunately brief—he was unable to move, and a less well-trained man would have lost consciousness. Yet as soon as Vostok reached its peak velocity of 17,500 mph, the engines were cut, and all sensation of weight vanished. Gagarin was in orbit, and was experiencing the unfamiliar sensation of zero gravity.

He was scheduled to make one orbit of the Earth, at a height ranging between 112 and 203 miles. He was busy all the time, so that he had little opportunity to relax and enjoy the view of the world far below—the first man ever to see it from such an altitude. Then, after one circuit, Vostok was slowed down by its retro-rockets and dropped back into the atmosphere, decreasing in speed until it was safe to open the parachutes. Gagarin landed safely in the pre-arranged point at 07.55 GMT. The total flight time had been one hour forty-eight minutes.

Today, when space-flights have become common, it does not sound remarkable; but remember that Gagarin had achieved something entirely new. Nobody had had any real idea of how a man's body would

react to zero gravity, and there had been suggestions that the result would be violent space-sickness; neither was it certain that the danger from meteoritic particles would be as slight as it has turned out to be. There were still people who claimed that space-travel would never be possible. Gagarin showed that this was not so.

He never made another journey beyond the atmosphere, but he was of immense help in other ways. I first met him in 1962, and I was enormously impressed by his easy manner and his obvious courage and sincerity. I remember, too, asking him whether he hoped to go to the Moon. He paused, and then replied: "If I am chosen, there will be no problem."

Sadly, it was not to be. In 1968 he took off on a normal routine aircraft flight, and crashed to his death. The whole world mourned him. He was a true hero, and a worthy first man in space.

SIR MARTIN RYLE
THE DEPTHS OF THE UNIVERSE

Martin Ryle, one of the greatest pioneers in the story of radio astronomy, was born in 1918, and graduated from Oxford in 1939. On the outbreak of war he became involved in the development of radar, which proved to be of such vital importance in the fight against Germany, and subsequently he went on to Cambridge, where he became the first Cambridge University Professor of Radio Astronomy. By then his reputation was world-wide. He was knighted in 1966, and six years later was appointed Astronomer Royal in succession to Sir Richard Woolley.

His first major research concerned radio waves from the Sun. For this he used a special type of radio telescope known as an interferometer. He studied not only the Sun, but also distant sources, identifying several—no easy task at that time, because the resolving power of early radio telescopes was poor, and two sources lying side by side tended to merge into one. Ryle went on to develop the technique of "aperture synthesis", which involves using several small instruments—some of them movable—to act in the same way that a very large radio telescope would do. He then led the team which drew up the classic Cambridge catalogues of radio sources.

Meanwhile, there had been new discussions about the origin of the universe. A group of Cambridge astronomers—initially Herman Bondi and Thomas Gold, later joined by Sir Fred Hoyle — had put forward the so-called steady-state theory, according to which the universe has always existed, and will exist for ever. There was no "big bang" and no beginning. Ryle disagreed, and he found a way to check the theory. If the universe were in a

Radio aerials at the Mullard Radio Astronomy Observatory at Cambridge (1978).

steady state, then conditions long ago must have been the same as they are now. Emissions from very remote objects will be recorded not as they are today, but as they used to be; for example, emissions from an object at a distance of 10 million light-years will show the object as it was 10 million years ago. What Ryle was doing, in effect, was to look back into the past, which is the next best thing to time-travel. He found that there were important differences; the distribution of faint radio sources was not the same as it is closer to us. Therefore the universe is not in a steady state, and the whole theory is wrong.

It was most unfortunate that the results were learned by a London science journalist before Ryle had officially announced them, so that the supporters of the steady-state theory first read them in the daily press. This led to considerable ill-feeling, but it was in no way Ryle's fault. He did not realize that not all journalists can be trusted.

In his later years he suffered from ill-health, and was succeeded as Astronomer Royal by another great radio astronomer, Sir Francis Graham Smith, the present holder of the office. Ryle himself died in 1984 after a long illness.

Martin Ryle was a great man in everyway. He disliked public speaking, and was always nervous before appearing on television; he joined me on several occasions in the *Sky at Night* programme, but I was reluctant to ask him more often, because I knew that although he would always agree to appear he would not enjoy it. The fact that he would always help in every possible way was a sure indication of his kindness and generosity.

BEYOND THE GALAXY

In following the story of astronomy, we have seen that many ideas which have been regarded as firmly established have had to be rejected in the end. Can this also be true of the distance-scale of our entire universe? Some astronomers believe so.

Quasars hold the key to the problem. As we have seen, they are generally thought to be very remote and super-luminous; the present holder of the "distance record" is PKS 2000-330, whose distance is estimated at 13,000 million light-years, and which is apparently receding at over 90 per cent of the velocity of light. If Hubble's Law holds good out to still greater distances, then the limit of the observable universe may lie at little more than 15,000 million light-years, since at this distance an object would be racing away at the full speed of light and we would be unable to see it.

The discovery of quasars—or, rather, their identification—was remarkable. One of the radio sources, 3C-273 (the 273rd entry in the third Cambridge catalogue) happened to lie in a position in which it could be occulted by the Moon. This meant that it could be pinpointed very accurately, and identified with what looked like a faint bluish star. In 1963 Maarten Schmidt used the Hale 200-inch reflector at Palomar to examine the optical spectrum of 3C-273, and was baffled inasmuch as the spectral lines did not seem to correspond with anything at all. Finally he discovered that they were due to hydrogen, but immensely redshifted, which indicated great distance and

(*Below*) *Centaurus A, nearest of the large radio galaxies, as photographed with the 200-inch Palomar reflector. It was once believed to consist of two galaxies which were in collision—that is to say, passing through each other—but it is now believed to be a single galaxy of unusual form.*

(*Right*) *The Magellanic Clouds of Nuberculæ in the far south of the sky. They lie within 200,000 light-years of us, and are the nearest large systems, though both are much smaller than our Galaxy. They are irregular in form, though indications of spirality have been claimed for the Large Cloud.*

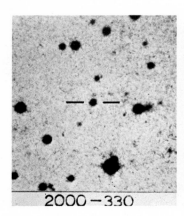

2000 — 330

(*Above*) *The quasar PKS 2000-330.
It was identified at the Parkes radio
astronomy observatory in New South
Wales, and optically confirmed at the
Siding Spring Observatory. It is here
shown in the centre of the plate
(which is a negative), indicated by
the two markers.*
(*Right*) *Spiral galaxy in Sculptor.
Photographed with the 48-inch
Schmidt telescope, Palomar.*

(*Above*) *Cluster of galaxies.*

almost unbelievably high luminosity.

But are the red shifts reliable as distance-indicators? One doubter is Professor Sir Fred Hoyle, one of the most celebrated of modern astronomers. He has made fundamental contributions to astrophysics and cosmology, and even though the "steady-state" theory which he supported has now been rejected it was still of immense value in stimulating research. Hoyle is convinced that the quasars are not nearly so remote as their red shifts indicate, and he is impressed by the work of H C Arp, who has found apparent associations between galaxies and quasars which have very different red shifts. According to Hoyle, some of the quasars may be reasonably local to our Galaxy.

This is still a minority view, but Hoyle is

not alone; he is supported by some eminent authorities—and he is one of those people who is quite capable of being right when almost everyone else is wrong. If he is right about the quasars, then the whole of modern cosmology will have to be re-cast. We may not have to go back to Square One, but we will certainly have to return to Square Two.

Time will tell. But the whole problem is yet another reminder that although we have learned so much, we are still very uncertain about some of the fundamental facts. The "men of the stars" who will carry on the story during the coming centuries have a great deal to do.

(Above) The barred spiral galaxy NGC 7741 (200-inch reflector, Palomar). The arms come from a sort of "bar" through the centre of the system.

(Above) The irregular galaxy Messier 82 in Ursa Major. It is a strong radio source, and was once believed to show indications of a tremendous central explosion, though this is not now thought to be the case.

THE SPACE-TRAVELLERS

(**Left**) Alan Shepard, the first American in space. On 5 May 1961 he blasted off from Cape Canaveral, and reached an altitude of 116 miles; the trip lasted for just over 15 minutes, and his capsule landed in the sea some 300 miles away from the launching site.
(**Below**) Yuri Gagarin, the first of all space-men, whose flight in Vostok I, in 1959, may be said to have opened the age of manned space exploration.

The real Space Age began only in 1957, but the idea itself goes back much earlier. In the second century AD the Greek satirist Lucian of Samosata wrote a story about a voyage to the Moon which he called the *True History* because, in his own words, it was made up of nothing but lies from beginning to end. Much later, even Johannes Kepler wrote a story about a lunar journey, though his hero was carried Moonward by demons rather than by rocket power.

Actually, the first really scientific description of space travel was given by a shy, deaf Russian teacher named Konstantin Tsiolkovskii, in the 1890s. In particular, he realized that a rocket functions by the principle of reaction, so that it is at its best in empty space. For years his work was almost unknown, though it was recognized by the Kremlin before his death in 1934. Another pioneer was a German, Hermann Gans-windt, who also grasped the main principle, though his proposed space vehicle sounds a little dangerous—it involved using gunpowder to power a sort of piston effect. (He also invented various other devices, such as a helicopter which might even have worked if only he had been able to provide it with an engine.)

The first liquid-propellant rocket was due to an American, Robert Hutchings Goddard, in 1926. He too was a curious character, and he had a marked dislike of the Press, mainly because he had been ridiculed in 1918 when he dared to suggest that it might be possible to send a rocket to the Moon. Slightly earlier than Goddard's rocket, the Romanian mathematician Hermann Oberth had published the first really scientific treatise on the subject, *The Rocket into Interplanetary Space*. I have met Oberth, though we had no common language. I gather that his political creed was rather to

the Right of that of Genghis Khan!

In the 1930s a group of German researchers set up a rocket proving ground near Berlin. One of its leaders was Wernher von Braun, probably the outstanding figure of early "astronautics". When the Nazis took over, they transferred the experimenters to Peenemünde, an island in the Baltic, and from here came the V2 weapons which did so much damage to London in the last stages of the war. Subsequently, von Braun and his colleagues transferred to the United States, and it was von Braun who was responsible for launching America's first artificial satellite, Explorer 1, in 1958. During the war, the Royal Air Force bombed Peenemünde. I was not on that raid, though I might well have been. Less than ten years later, I was

(**Below**) Dr Harrison ("Jack") Schmitt, who went to the Moon in Apollo 17—the first trained geologist to do so.

(**Below**) Valentina Tereshkova, the first woman in space, who flew in Russia's Vostok 6 in June 1963.

having a very friendly dinner with von Braun in the United States!

After the flight of Sputnik 1, even the doubters had to realize that space-flight was practicable. The first cosmonaut was, of course, Yuri Gagarin. He was followed less than a month later by Alan Shepard, though it is true that Shepard's flight was a sub-orbital "hop" lasting only a quarter of an hour. I listened to his commentary from my study in Sussex, and I also commented on television during the later flight of Apollo 14, when Shepard landed on the Moon. This, surely, shows the rapidity of progress in those days.

The first man on the Moon was Neil Armstrong, in July 1969—surely the ideal representative of Earth, and someone I am proud to know. The last man on the Moon—so far—was Commander Eugene Cernan, who flew with Apollo 17 in 1972. I was interested when he told me that the most vivid, last-ing impression he has was the view of our own Earth from a distance of a quarter of a million miles. He believes, too, that we will go back as soon as we have real motivation. "I believe we'll go to Mars, too," he said to me during a television programme. "If the Viking landers had shown little green men with long ears looking back at us, we'd be on our way to Mars now."

The first decades of the Space Age were pioneering. We may now be ready for a period of consolidation, and there is every chance that during the 1990s there will be permanently manned space-stations which will be of immense value to all mankind. We may even have a fully-fledged Lunar Base before the year 2000—always provided that we do not indulge in another futile war which would destroy everything that has been built up since the dawn of civilization.

(**Below**) The first men round the Moon, in December 1968—the men of Apollo 8—Frank Borman, James Lovell and William Anders.

The Apollo programme began in the early 1960s, when President John F. Kennedy committed the United States to putting a man on the Moon before the end of the decade. The unmanned Orbiters provided excellent maps of the entire lunar surface (thereby finishing off the programme which François Arago, in 1840, had estimated would take no more than a few minutes), and the Luna and Surveyor soft-landings have finally proved that Gold's deep-dust theory was wrong. Then came the first circum-lunar manned flights, first by Apollo 8 and then by Apollo 10 (Apollo 9 was an Earth-orbiter, during which the lunar module was given its first real test in space). The stage was set, and on 16 July 1969 Apollo 11, carrying Neil Armstrong, Edwin Aldrin and Michael Collins, blasted off from Cape

Canaveral.

All three had been in space during the Gemini flights of 1966; Armstrong in Gemini 8, Collins in Gemini 10 and Aldrin in Gemini 12. Armstrong's flight had not been smooth. Gemini 8 had carried out a successful docking operation with an unmanned Agena rocket which had been put into orbit to act as a target, but 20 minutes later the space-craft began to roll and yaw because of what was later found to be a fault in the electrical system. It took Armstrong and his co-pilot, David Scott, some time to stop the tumbling motion by using power bursts from the rocket motor designed for use during the return to Earth. They then succeeded in separating Gemini 8 from the Agena, and landed safely, though some five hundred miles east of the planned area. Had Armstrong

and Scott been less well-trained, and less cool, the emergency would certainly have turned into a tragedy. Aldrin, in the last vehicle of the Gemini series, had spent well over two hours outside the capsule, coping with the conditions remarkably well.

Millions of people were watching when *Eagle*, the lunar module of Apollo 11, dropped down toward the lunar surface on the night of 20-21 July 1969 (night, that is to say, in Britain, where I was in the BBC television studio carrying out a live commentary). After all, the astronauts were tackling something new. Suppose we had been wrong, and that treacherous areas really did exist? There was no chance of rescue in the event of a faulty landing, and this was probably the greatest weakness in the whole Apollo concept. At the last moment Armstrong had to manœuvre *Eagle* down-range

to avoid a crater "the size of a football pitch"; then, when his voice came through to say "The *Eagle* has landed", one could sense the feeling of relief everywhere. It was certainly shared by two of the great pioneers, Hermann Oberth and Wernher von Braun, who were watching from Mission Control. Things had moved fast since the days when Oberth wrote his classic book and van Braun was experimenting at the primitive rocket proving ground outside Berlin. (Incidentally, do you realize that Armstrong could have met Orville Wright, the first flyer? Wright lived until 1948; I met him in 1940, when I was myself learning how to fly in the earlier stages of the war.)

At 01.53 GMT on 21 July the *Eagle's* cabin was depressurized. Half an hour later the "personal life support systems" were switched on; the hatch was

opened, and Armstrong made his way down the ladder. At 02.55 he reached the footpad, and paused briefly before stepping out on to the bleak Sea of Tranquillity. "That's one small step for a man, one giant leap for mankind."

Aldrin joined him a few minutes later. He was an Army colonel (Armstrong was a civilian) and was essentially practical, but I doubt whether anyone has bettered his description of the lunar scene, which he called "magnificent desolation".

And what about the third member of the Apollo 11 crew, Michael Collins? Let nobody underestimate his part in the mission. Without him it could not have been carried through, even though he did not actually set foot on the Moon. He was typically unselfish about it; after all, as he said, he had gone more than 90 per cent of the way.

Apollo 11 can never be forgotten. Some months after the end of the mission I was talking to Armstrong, and asked him whether he thought a lunar base could be built. "I'm quite certain that we'll have such bases in our lifetime," he said. "There are no storms, no snow, no high winds, no unpredictable weather; as for the gravity— well, the Moon's a very pleasant

kind of place to work in; better than Earth." And Neil

*(**Above, left**) Neil Armstrong in the capsule of Eagle, while it was on the Moon. (**Above, right**) Edwin Aldrin surveys the American flag which has been set up; in the absence of air, the flag does not flutter. (**Left**) Aldrin stands on the Moon, with the entire scene reflected in the transparent facepiece of his helmet.*

Armstrong, of all people, ought to know!

One problem about space-flight during the first period was its cost. A rocket could be used only once, which was rather like building a new locomotive for every train journey between London and Glasgow. What was needed was a vehicle which could be used over and over again. It was finally achieved with the Space Shuttle.

It has been said that the Shuttle takes off like a rocket, flies like a space-ship and lands like a glider, which is a fair description. It took a long time to develop—much longer than had been originally expected—and this gave the false impression that the American space programme was slowing down. At last, in 1981, all was ready, and Columbia, the first Shuttle, was launched on 12 April, twenty years after Yuri Gagarin's classic single orbit of the Earth. The Shuttle pilot was John Young, who had been to the Moon with Apollo 16; his co-pilot was Robert Crippen, making his first trip into space.

Four more flights with Columbia took place before the next Shuttle, Challenger, lifted off on 5 April 1983. Of the Columbia crews, two men had special claims to be remembered. The commander of Columbia's second flight (12 November 1981) was Colonel Joe Engle, who had originally been selected to fly to the Moon with Apollo 17, but had been taken out so that he could make way for the professional geologist, Dr Schmitt. It must have been a bitter disappointment, but Columbia made up for it to some extent (just as Deke Slayton, the only one of the "original seven" astronauts who did not fly in the early days, went into space in 1972 on a link-up mission with the Russians).

The second Shuttle, Chal-

lenger, was commanded by Paul Weitz, more than ten years after his dramatic experience with Skylab. In other Shuttle missions there have been Spacelab stations, which are not independent but are carried in the Shuttle bay. Women have flown them, and observers and crews have come from many nations to take part in certain missions. We may still be a long way from the time when it will be conventional to take "holidays" in space", but tremendous advances have been made, and there have been some unusual missions—as for instance the orbital repair of an ailing satellite, Solar Maximum Mission, which was literally captured, taken on board the Shuttle, repaired and re-launched. It was during this venture that Astronaut Bruce McCandless became the first "free flyer", unattached to his space-ship by any safety cord.

It was all the more unexpected when, in January 1986, tragedy struck. The 25th Shuttle flight—with the Challenger—was carrying seven astronauts; after what seemed to be a routine blast-off it exploded, killing all the crew. The shock and sadness was felt all round the world. We can only hope that such a disaster will never happen again. As President Reagan said, the seven Challenger astronauts gave their lives for humanity; they will never be forgotten.

(*Left*) The Shuttle being launched. The first Shuttle astronauts: (left) John Young, who had flown to the Moon with Apollo 16, and (right) Robert Crippen, making his first journey into space.

(*Above*) The Shuttle in orbit; the Earth is far below, and the vehicle is flying in its "space-ship" mode. When it lands, it will be converted into what may be termed a massive glider.

TIME-CHART

114

1729	Hall discovers the principle of the achromatic object-glass.
1744	Brilliant comet observed by de Chéseaux and others.
1750	Lacaille begins his catalogue of the southern stars. Wright publishes his *Original Theory*.
1758	Halley's Comet recovered, by Palitzsch.
1761	Transit of Venus; atmosphere of the planet discovered by Lomonosov.
1762	Bradley published his star catalogue.
1767	Maskelyne founds the *Nautical Almanac*.
1769	Transit of Venus extensively observed.
1776	Small but good lunar map published by T. Mayer.
1779	Schröter founds his observatory at Lilienthal.
1781	Herschel discovers Uranus.
1783	Goodricke explains the variations of Algol.
1784	Goodricke discovers the variability of Delta Cephei.
1786	Herschel's speculations about the shape of the Galaxy.
1789	Herschel completes his 49-inch reflector, and with it discovers Mimas and Enceladus.
1796	Publication of Laplace's Nebular Hypothesis.
1800	Solar infra-red radiation discovered by Herschel. "Celestial Police" founded at Lilienthal.
1801	Piazzi discovers Ceres. Wollaston observes dark lines in the solar spectrum. Herschel shows that many double stars are true binaries.
1802	Olbers discovers Pallas.
1803	Meteorite fall at L'Aigle in France; meteorites shown to come from space.
1804	Harding discovers Juno.
1807	Olbers discovers Vesta.
1811	Brilliant Comet observed.
1813	Schröter's observatory destroyed by French soldiers.
1815	Fraunhofer publishes his map of the solar spectrum.

1818	Encke predicts the return of a comet discovered by Pons.
1820	Foundation of the Royal Astronomical Society.
1822	Encke's Comet recovered.
1824	First clock-driven telescope (at Dorpat Observatory).
1826	Biela's Comet discovered.
1833	Brilliant Leonid meteor shower.
1834	John Herschel goes to the Cape, and between then and 1838 makes the first full survey of the southern sky.
1835	Return of Halley's Comet.
1837	Beer and Mädler publish their great book about the Moon.
1838	Bessel measures the distance of a star (61 Cygni).
1840	First photograph of the Moon taken, by Draper.
1843	First photograph of the solar spectrum, by Draper.
1843	Schwabe announces the discovery of the 11-year solar cycle. Brilliant comet observed.
1844	Harvard College Observatory founded.
1845	Lord Rosse completes his 72-inch reflector, and discovers the spiral forms of the galaxies. Hencke discovers the fifth asteroid, Astræa.
1846	Discovery of Neptune, by Galle and D'Arrest. Discovery of Triton, by Lassell.
1850	Discovery of Saturn's Crêpe Ring, by Bond. First photographs of stars (Castor and Vega).
1852	Last appearance of Biela's Comet.
1858	Appearance of the brilliant Donati's Comet.
1859	Interpretation of the dark lines in the Sun's spectrum, by Kirchhoff and Bunsen.
1861	Brilliant comet observed.
1862	Discovery of the Companion of Sirius, by Clark. Publication of the *Bonner Durchmusterung*, by Argelander.
1863	Secchi classifies the stars into definite spectral types.
1864	Huggins proves that some nebulæ are gaseous.

1865 Publication of Jules Verne's novel *From the Earth to the Moon*.

1866 Brilliant Leonid meteor shower.

1868 Janssen and Lockyer show how to observe solar prominences without waiting for an eclipse.

1870 First photograph of a solar prominence (by Young).

1874 Transit of Venus widely observed.
Meudon Observatory founded.

1877 Schiaparelli describes the Martian canals.
Phobos and Delmos discovered, by Hall.

1882 Gill photographs a bright comet, and realizes that photography is the best way to map the stars.
Transit of Venus, again widely observed.

1885 Appearance of a supernova in the Andromeda Spiral.

1887 Lick 36-inch refractor completed.

1888 Publication of Dreyer's *New General Catalogue* of clusters and nebulæ.

1889 First spectroscopic binaries discovered (Mizar and Beta Aurigæ).

1890 British Astronomical Association founded.
E C Pickering gives a new classification of stellar spectra.

1891 Spectroheliograph invented, by Hale and Deslandres.
First photographic discovery of an asteroid, by Max Wolf.

1892 Barnard discovers Amalthea.
First photographic discovery of a comet.

1894 Lowell founds his observatory at Flagstaff, in Arizona.
First scientific article about space-flight, by Tsiolkovskii.

1896 Meudon 33-inch refractor completed.

1897 Yerkes Observatory completed.

1898 Witt discovers Eros, the first asteroid to come within the orbit of Mars.

1901 Brilliant nova seen in Perseus.

1903 Tsiolkovskii publishes his most important paper about rockets.

1905 Mount Wilson Observatory founded.

1908 Giant and dwarf classes of stars described, by Hertzsprung.
Mount Wilson 60-inch reflector completed.
Fall of the Siberian missile.

1910 Return of Halley's Comet.

1911 First HR Diagrams drawn.

1912 Discovery of the Cepheid period-luminosity law, by Miss Leavitt.

1913 Russell publishes his theory of stellar evolution.

1914 First practical rocket experiments, by Goddard.

1915 Companion of Sirius discovered, by W S Adams.

1917 Mount Wilson 100-inch reflector completed.

1918 Shapley gives his estimate for the size of the Galaxy.
Brilliant nova seen in Aquila.

1919 Catalogue of dark nebulæ published, by Barnard.

1920 Slipher publishes his results about the red shifts in the spectra of galaxies.
"Great Debate" between Shapley and Curtis about the size of the Galaxy and the status of the spiral nebulæ.

1923 Hubble proves that the galaxies are external systems.

1924 Oberth publishes his classic book *The Rocket into Interplanetary Space*.

1926 First liquid-propellant rocket fired, by Goddard.

1927 Foundation of the first important German rocket society.

1930 Clyde Tombaugh discovers Pluto.
Bernhard Schmidt invents the Schmidt telescope.

1931 Jansky detects radio waves from the Milky Way.

1932 Dunham discovers carbon dioxide in the atmosphere of Venus.

1937 Grote Reber builds the first intentional radio telescope.

1938 Bethe and Gamow publish the new theory of stellar evolution.

1942 Radio waves from the Sun detected, by Hey.

1944 Kuiper discovers the atmosphere of Titan.
Van de Hulst proposes the 21-cm radiation from clouds of hydrogen in the Galaxy.

1946 Preliminary work at Jodrell Bank.
Cygnus A radio source identified, by Ryle and Smith.

1948 Palomar 200-inch reflector completed.
Steady-state theory of the universe proposed (by Gold and Bondi).

1949 Identification of other radio sources, including the Crab Nebula.
Rocket testing ground established at Cape Canaveral.

1951 21-cm radiation discovered by Ewen and Purcelli.

1952 Baade announces the revision of the distance-scale for the galaxies.

1955 Jodrel Bank 250-ft radio telescope completed.
First radio interferometer constructed, by Ryle.

1957 Russia launches Sputnik 1, thus opening the Space Age.

1959 First successful lunar probes (the Russian Luniks).
Far side of the Moon photographed.

1961 Parkes 210-ft radio telescope completed.
First Venus probe (Russia's Venera 1; unsuccessful).
First man in space (Gagarin).
First American in space (Shepard, sub-orbital "hop".

1962 First successful planetary probe: Mariner 2, to Venus.
First American in space orbit (Glenn).
First Transatlantic television relay satellite (Telstar).
Discovery of the first cosmic X-ray source (Scorpius X-1).

1963 M. Schmidt identifies quasars.

1964 First really good close-range lunar photographs, from Ranger 7.

1965 First "space-walk" (by Alexei Leonov).
Mars photographed from Mariner 4.
Microwave radiation from space detected by Penzias and Wilson.

1966 First automatic soft landing on the Moon (Luna 9).

1967 J. Bell-Burnell discovers pulsars.
98-inch Isaac Newton reflector set up at Herstmonceux.

1968 Vela pulsar identified as a radio source.
First manned flight round the Moon (Apollo 8).

1969 Armstrong and Aldrin land on the Moon, from Apollo 11.
Crab pulsar identified optically, by Taylor and Disney.
Gamma-ray source identified in the sky.

1970 Great new reflectors completed at Cerro Tololo (Chile), Kitt Peak (Arizona) and Mauna Kea (Hawaii).
Venera 7 makes a controlled landing on Venus.

1971 Launch of Uhuru, the X-ray satellite.

1971 Improved photographs of Mars obtained from Mariner 9.
End of the Apollo programme, with Apollo 12.

1973 First Skylab mission (the programme was completed in 1974).
Pioneer 10 by-passes Jupiter.

1974 Pioneer 11 by-passes Jupiter.
Mercury photographed from Mariner 10.

1975 Combined USSR-USA space mission (Apollo/Soyuz).
Veneras 9 and 10 send back pictures from the surface of Venus.

1976 First controlled landings on Mars (Vikings 1 and 2).
Russian 236-inch reflector completed.

1977 C. Kowal discovers Chiron.
Rings of Uranus discovered.
Voyagers 1 and 2 launched.

1978 Christy discovers Charon, the satellite of Pluto.
First reliable maps of Venus, from Pioneer 12.

1979 Two fly-by missions to Jupiter (Voyagers 1 and 2).
First fly-by of Saturn (Pioneer 11).
La Palma Observatory opened.
UKIRT completed on Mauna Kea.

1980 Voyager 1 sends back close-range pictures of Saturn.

1981 Second fly-by of Saturn (Voyager 2).
First successful tests of the Space Shuttle.

1983 New infra-red studies from IRAS, including the discovery of cool material associated with several stars such as Vega and Fomalhaut.

1985 Mount Wilson 100-inch reflector taken out of service.

1986 Return of Halley's Comet.
Voyager 2 flies past Uranus.

GLOSSARY

Albedo The reflecting power of a non-luminous body. A perfect reflector would have an albedo of 100 per cent.

Ångström unit The hundred-millionth part of a centimetre.

Antoniadi scale A roman numeral indicates the quality of the seeing according to the following scale:

  I Perfect seeing, without a quiver

 II Slight undulations, with moments of calm lasting several seconds

III Moderate seeing, with larger air tremors

IV Poor seeing, with constant troublesome undulations

 V Very bad seeing, scarcely allowing the making of a rough sketch

Aperture The diameter of an opening through which light passes in an optical instrument.

Aphelion The furthest distance of a planet from the Sun.

Apparent magnitude The apparent brightness of a celestial object: the lower the magnitude, the brighter the object.

Aurora (Polar Lights) A diffuse glow in the upper air caused by electrified particles emitted from the Sun.

Axis An imaginary line about which a body rotates. The polar diameter of a planet is the axis of rotation.

Binary Two stars that move around their common centre of gravity.

Black hole The remains of a massive star after its final collapse and contraction into a state where the gravitational pull is so strong that not even light can escape.

Caldera A volcanic crater.

Celestial sphere An imaginary sphere surrounding the Earth, concentric with the Earth's centre.

Cepheid variable A variable star of short period. The fluctuations are regular and are linked with its real luminosity; the longer the period, the more luminous the star.

Chromosphere That part of the Sun's atmosphere that lies just above its visible surface or photosphere.

Circumpolar star A star that never sets. Ursa Major, for example, is circumpolar over the British Isles, and Crux Australis is circumpolar over New Zealand.

Conjunction (1) A planet is said to be in conjunction with a star when it is apparently close to it in the sky. (2) The planets within the Earth's orbit, Mercury and Venus, are at inferior conjunction when lined up between Earth and Sun and at superior conjunction when on the far side of the Sun. It follows that Mars and the other planets outside the Earth's orbit can reach only superior conjunction.

Constellation A group of stars within an imaginary outline.

Corona The outermost part of the Sun's atmosphere. Made up of very thin gas, it is invisible to the maked eye except during a total eclipse.

Cosmology The study of the universe.

Culmination The maximum altitude of a celestial body.

Declination The angular distance of a celestial body from the celestial equator.

Density The quantity of matter contained within a unit of volume.

Direct motion The movement of a celestial body from west to east, that is, in the same direction as that of the Earth, around the Sun.

Doppler Effect The apparent change in the wavelength of light according to the motion of the body emitting it, in relation to the observer's position. With an approaching light source the wavelength is shortened ("too blue"), with a receding source it is lengthened ("too red").

Double star A pair of stars. A double may be caused by a genuine physical association (when it is known as a binary star) or by an optical effect: two stars appearing to be close together but in fact just happening to lie in almost exactly the same line when seen from Earth.

Eccentricity The measure of how well a planet's orbit compares with a perfect circle.

Eclipse, lunar The passage of the Moon through the shadow cast by the Earth. Lunar eclipses may be either total or partial.

Eclipse, solar The covering of the Sun by the Moon, when seen from Earth. Solar eclipses may be either total, partial or annular. An annular eclipse occurs when the Moon is close to its point of maximum recession from the Earth and so is too small to hide the Sun completely.

Eclipsing binary A binary star, one component of which is seen to pass in front of the other, thereby cutting out some or all of its light.

Ecliptic The apparent yearly path of the Sun against the stars.

Elongation The angular distance of a planet from the Sun or of a satellite from its primary planet.

Equator, celestial The projection of the Earth's equator on to the celestial sphere, thus dividing the sky into equal hemispheres.

Equinox The two points at which the Sun crosses the celestial equator; the spring equinox (first point of Aries) is reached about 21 March and the autumnal equinox about 22 September.

Escape velocity The minimum velocity that an object must possess to escape from the surface of a planet or other body.

Extinction The apparent reduction in the brightness of a star or planet when low over the horizon because more of its light is absorbed by the Earth's atmosphere.

Eyepiece The lens (or lenses) at the eye end of a telescope responsible for enlarging the image produced by the object-glass (for a refractor) or mirror (for a reflector).

Faculae The bright patches on the Sun's photosphere.

Finder A small, wide-field telescope attached to a larger one for locating objects in the sky.

Flare, solar Brilliant outbreaks in the solar atmosphere normally detectable only by spectroscopic methods.

Flare star A faint red star that has short-lived explosions on its surface. These explosions cause the star to appear temporarily brighter.

Fraunhofer lines The dark lines in the spectrum of the Sun.

Galaxy A star system. Most galaxies are so remote that their light takes millions of years to reach Earth.

Inclination Measure of the tilt of a planet's orbital plane, in relation to that of the Earth's.

Inferior planet Any planet that orbits between the Sun and the Earth; ie Mercury and Venus.

Libration An effect caused by the apparent slight "wobbling" of the Moon from side to side, as seen from Earth. As a result a total of 59 per cent of the Moon's surface can be observed although no more than 50 per cent at any time. The remaining 41 per cent remained unknown to observers from Earth until the Space Age explorations.

Light-year The distance travelled by light in one year: that is to say 9.46 million million kilometres.

Limb An edge or border, as of the Sun, Moon or any planet.

Local Group The group of which our Galaxy is a member. There are more than two dozen systems, including the Andromeda Spiral and the two Clouds of Magellan.

Luminosity The amount of light emitted from a star.

Lunation The interval between one new Moon and the next, that is to say 29 days 12 hours 44 minutes.

Magnetosphere The area around a planet in which its magnetic field is dominant.

Magnitude The measure of the apparent brightness of a celestial object. The lower the magnitude, the brighter the object.

Meridian An imaginary circle through the north and south poles of the celestial sphere.

Meteor A small particle that burns away in the Earth's upper air. It is often known as a shooting star.

Meteorite A natural body, probably associated with asteroids, which is able to reach ground level without being destroyed.

Nebula A cloud of dust and gas in space, from which fresh stars are created.

Neutron A fundamental particle with no electrical charge.

Neutron star A star made up principally, or completely, of neutrons. Theoretically, it is the remnant of a massive star that has exploded. Neutron stars that send out rapidly varying radio waves are known as pulsars.

Nova A star that suddenly flares up to many times its normal brightness and remains brilliant for a limited period before fading back to obscurity.

Object-glass (or Objective) The main lens in a refracting telescope.

Oblateness The degree of flattening at the poles of a celestial body.

Occultation The concealment of one celestial body by another. Strictly speaking, a solar eclipse is an occultation of the Sun by the Moon.

Opposition The position of a planet when exactly opposite the Sun in the sky, as seen from Earth. The planet is then best placed for observation.

Orbit The path of a celestial body.

Parallax The apparent shift in position of an object when viewed from two different positions.

Perihelion The closest point that a planet (or other body) comes to the Sun.

Periodic time *see* Sidereal period.

Phase The apparent change in the shape of the Moon and inferior planets, according to the amount of sunlit hemisphere turned towards the Earth. New Moon, for example, is when the unlit side of the Moon is visible. Full Moon is when its surface is fully exposed as viewed from Earth.

Photosphere The brilliant visible surface of the Sun.

Planetary nebula A small, hot star surrounded by a shell of gas.

Poles, celestial The north and south points of the celestial sphere.

Precession The apparent slow movement of the celestial poles caused by a real shift in the direction of the Earth's axis.

Prominence A mass of glowing gas, chiefly hydrogen, above the Sun's photosphere.

Pulsar *see* Neutron star.

Quasar A very remote, super-luminous object. The nature of a quasar is still uncertain.

Radial velocity The movement of a celestial body towards or away from the observer.

Radiant The point in the sky from which a meteor shower appears to emanate.

Red giant The stage in the evolution of an ordinary star when the core contracts, the surface expands to about 50 solar radii and its temperature drops, giving the star its red colour.

Retrograde motion The movement of a celestial body from east to west; that is, in the opposite direction to that of the Earth.

Right ascension The time that elapses between the culmination of the First Point of Aries and the culmination of a celestial body.

Seyfert galaxy A galaxy that has a small, bright nucleus and faint spiral arms. It is often a strong radio source.

Sidereal period The revolution period of a planet around the Sun or that of a satellite around its primary. Also known as Periodic Time.

Solar wind Charged particles from the Sun that travel into the Solar System at about 1½ million kph.

Spectroscopic binary A very close double that is only recognizable by its displacing effects in the combined spectrum of the two stars.

Spectrum The range of colour produced by a prism.

Supergiant The stage in the evolution of a massive star when the core contracts, the surface expands and the temperature drops, giving the star its red colour.

Superior planet Any planet beyond the orbit of the Earth in the Solar System.

Supernova A massive star that reaches a peak of luminosity and then explodes in a cataclasmic outburst and dies, leaving a neutron star surrounded by a cloud of expanding gas.

Synodic period The interval between successive oppositions of a superior planet.

Terminator The boundary between the illuminated and dark portions of a planet or satellite.

Transit The passage of a celestial body across the observer's meridian; the apparent passage of a small body across the disk of a larger one.

Van Allen Belts Radiation zones of charged particles surrounding the Earth.

Variable star A star that fluctuates in brilliancy. Eclipsing binaries are categorized under this heading.

White dwarf A small, very dense star that has used up its nuclear energy and collapsed. White dwarfs have been described as "bankrupt stars".

Yellow dwarf An ordinary star such as the Sun at a comparatively stable and long-lived stage in its evolution.

Zenith The observer's overhead point (latitude 90°).

Zodiac A belt stretching 8° to either side of the ecliptic, in which the Sun, Moon and all planets are always to be found.

Zodiacal Light A cone of light rising from the horizon after sunset or before sunrise. It is caused by sunlight on thinly spread inter-planetary material in the main plane of the Solar System.

INDEX